Chesterton's Gateway

14 Essays To Get You
Hooked On Chesterton

ESSAY SELECTIONS,
INTRODUCTIONS, FOOTNOTES
and ILLUSTRATIONS
by ETHAN NICOLLE

Contents

Introduction (page 5)

1: **Tremendous Trifles** (page 9)

2: **A Piece Of Chalk** (page 15)

3: **Introductory Remarks On The Importance Of Orthodoxy** (page 21)

4: **On Certain Modern Writers And The Institution Of The Family** (page 31)

5 **On Lying In Bed** (page 43)

6. **On Running After One's Hat** (page 49)

7. **Cheese** (page 55)

8. **The Medical Mistake** (page 59)

9. **The Maniac** (page 65)

10. **The Ethics Of Elfland** (page 85)

11. **The Paradoxes Of Christianity** (page 109)

12. **The Drift From Domesticity** (page 137)

13. **The Book Of Job** (page 147)

14. **What Is Right With The World** (page 159)

15. **Afterword** (page 171)

Introduction

Ever since I took up podcasting one of the most common questions I get asked is, "where should I start if I want to get into G.K. Chesterton?" My answer usually goes something like this: "Oh, well, Orthodoxy is tough to just dive into. His fiction is good but it might be better to read Tremendous Trifles—of course if you do that there are a lot of things you will miss out on, but Orthodoxy is hard and—bah! Let me just give you a list of essays to start with." Finally, I decided to just go ahead and make a book of my favorite Chesterton essays—especially the ones I would recommend to someone who is new to Chesterton.

Why essays? Shouldn't you read a full book cover to cover as the author intended? Of the many hats Chesterton wore, from poet to detective novelist to playwright and cartoonist, essayist was Chesterton's top-most hat. Most of his nonfiction books really are collections of essays, and most of his chapters could be read on their own. He was a master essayist, and you will find, like most Chesterton fans, that you do not end up having a favorite Chesterton book as much as you have a list of favorite essays.

What are my qualifications to put together a Chesterton book? Heck, I didn't even finish community college. I am no scholar. So I'm not going to attempt to write some kind of dissertation on why Chesterton is amazing and relevant to the modern age. If you are reading this, I assume your interest has already been piqued, probably by one of his many, many snappy quotes. Besides, there are better books already written on Chesterton. I recommend Dale Ahlquist's online essay "G. K. Chesterton: Who is this guy and why haven't I heard of him?", and his books *The Apostle of Common Sense* and *Common Sense 101*. These can all be found on **chesterton.org**.

I have founded two Chesterton reading groups in California, each growing to around 35 members—though my current group is still growing. I have read many of his books, several of them multiple times. I am not a scholar, and while I do know Chesterton better than the casual reader, I'm not super smart. That's why I think I'm highly qualified to be the guy who makes a book of Chesterton's most accessible essays. I am not a complicated thinker. I am not a history buff. I have not consumed mass amounts of literature (besides Chesterton, heh) So, you do not need to be some heavily-studied big-brain smarty-pants to love the essays I am going to share with you here.

Oh also, I'm not a Catholic. I just love Chesterton.

I hope these essays will act as a gateway drug (hence the clever title), leading you into a rabid lifelong GKC addiction.

Footnotes

Like with all of Chesterton's works, it isn't always going to be easy reading. There will be many references to history and his contemporaries that you are not familiar with. But fret not—I'm adding footnotes throughout the book to keep you from having to attempt a Wikipedia search for context. I have always wanted an annotated Chesterton book, so here it is. Though you should be warned, I am no historian, and I could have gotten some of these horribly wrong. This is just me Googling for you, so you can enjoy the book. I tried to be thorough in what I noted so that pretty much any historical thing that is not currently ubiquitous (or is just some weird England thing) has an annotation.

Paragraph Breaks

Another thing I am doing as editor of this book, is I am going to throw a few more paragraph breaks in. I don't know what was going on back in Chesterton's day but he didn't seem to hit the return key very often. He has paragraphs that go on for pages. Since this is a "Chesterton with training wheels" book, I am going to break up the big paragraphs so you aren't scared away by walls of text. If you are ever in a reading group with other people who are reading these essays from other sources (they're all free online after all), I apologize for the confusion.

Chesterton's Style

One more note before we dive in. Chesterton doesn't write like we are used to reading in the age of self-help books and books with titles like *Ten Ways To Find Purpose And Self-Confidence Through The Words Of Jesus*. He also doesn't write like your typical nonfiction writer. He doesn't start with an introductory paragraph that sums up his whole point, then repeat the point with bullet points. He doesn't follow a path. He doesn't just dump statistics.

Often, he will start somewhere in the vicinity of his idea and you will have to chase him to his point as he bounds around his thoughts like a child trying to pick a game to play at Chuck E. Cheese. Chesterton was an illustrator (another reason I feel a connection with the man), and in some ways he writes like one. He starts with scribbles and general shapes. He paints a picture. He is not laying out a diagram. He is sketching, rubbing, erasing, adding shadows, highlights. He's Bob Ross. Just watch it all come together.

Well, hopefully.

I will be the first to admit I have read many essays by Chesterton that left me clueless as to what his point was. My friend and coworker Kyle Mann will often finish reading a Chesterton essay and give it a "How High Was Chesterton When He Wrote This?" rating. I tried to leave his more esoteric writing out of this volume, but I'm sure you will come across sentences you find cryptic or confusing. For me, I learned enough about Chesterton's views through his writings that make sense to me to be hungry to dig deeper into the things he has written that make less sense. This is exactly why I started a Chesterton reading group — because as soon as you finish reading a chapter of Chesterton, you want to process it with someone, see if they caught something you didn't.

You may come to a chapter that just loses you. I put a couple of longer ones in here. If one essay becomes a slog, feel free to move onto the next! This is a sampler! A Chesterton cheese tray!

Another thing to keep in mind about Chesterton is that he is funny. The more you read him, the more you get his jokes. He loves absurdest humor.

He loves poking fun at stuffy and proper contemporaries who think they've achieved true enlightenment with their monocles and top hats.

I feel like I could write forever. I have so much I want to tell you about this author who has had such a huge impact on my life, but you came to read Chesterton, not read me talking about him, so let's dive in. I have written introductions to each chapter that I think you'll find light and easy to read. You don't have to read these, but they will be there to explain why I chose them, what you are in for, and to prepare you for any contextual stuff that will be good to understand before you dive in.

If you bought this book, I'm thrilled to be the guy who introduced you to Chesterton. There is more information at the end of the book if you are ready to submit yourself to a full-blown Chesterton addiction.

ETHAN NICOLLE

Tremendous Trifles

Tremendous Trifles (**1909**)

"The world will never starve for want of wonders;
but only for want of wonder."

THIS IS MY favorite essay by Chesterton. It's got a beautiful simplicity to it and it makes me wish Chesterton wrote more fairy tales. This is the introduction to his essay collection, also titled *Tremendous Trifles*, and a great introduction for this book as well.

This essay gets into possibly the biggest theme throughout Chesterton's work, and that is wonder. Chesterton is always coming back to man's need for wonder and his ugly habit of blinding himself to it, the importance of choosing to be small so that the world around you is big. The more you humble yourself, the more grand and glorious the world becomes, and even God is enlarged.

I don't want to give away much more. The only context you need here is that this is the introduction to another book, so keep that in mind when he starts speaking of "this book." He means the book *Tremendous Trifles*, which is a great book, and you should definitely read it.

Once upon a time there were two little boys who lived chiefly in the front garden, because their villa was a model one. The front garden was about the same size as the dinner table; it consisted of four strips of gravel, a square of turf with some mysterious pieces of cork standing up in the middle and one flower bed with a row of red daisies. One morning while they were at play in these romantic grounds, a passing individual, probably the milkman, leaned over the railing and engaged them in philosophical conversation.

The boys, whom we will call Paul and Peter, were at least sharply interested in his remarks. For the milkman (who was, I need say, a fairy) did his duty in that state of life by offering them in the regulation manner anything that they chose to ask for. And Paul closed with the offer with a business-like abruptness, explaining that he had long wished to be a giant that he might stride across continents and oceans and visit Niagara or the Himalayas in an afternoon dinner stroll.

The milkman producing a wand from his breast pocket, waved it in a hurried and perfunctory manner; and in an instant the model villa with its front garden was like a tiny doll's house at Paul's colossal feet. He went striding away with his head above the clouds to visit Niagara and the Himalayas. But when he came to the Himalayas, he found they were quite small and silly-looking, like the little cork rockery in the garden; and when he found Niagara it was no bigger than the tap turned on in the bathroom. He wandered round the world for several minutes trying to find something really large and finding everything small, till in sheer boredom he lay down on four or five prairies and fell asleep.

Unfortunately his head was just outside the hut of an intellectual backwoodsman who came out of it at that moment with an axe in one hand and a book of Neo-Catholic Philosophy[1] in the other. The man looked at the book and then at the giant, and then at the book again. And in the book it said, "It can be maintained that the evil of pride consists in being out of proportion to the universe." So the backwoodsman put down his book, took his axe and, working eight hours a day for about a week, cut the giant's head off; and there was an end of him.

Such is the severe yet salutary history of Paul. But Peter, oddly enough, made exactly the opposite request; he said he had long wished to be a pigmy about half an inch high; and of course he immediately became one. When the transformation was over he found himself in the midst of an immense plain, covered with a tall green jungle and above which, at intervals, rose strange trees each with a head like the sun in symbolic pictures, with gigantic rays of silver and a huge heart of gold. Toward the middle of this prairie stood up a mountain of such romantic and impossible shape, yet of such stony height and dominance, that it looked like some incident of the end of the world. And far away on the faint horizon he could see the line of another forest, taller and yet more mystical, of a terrible crimson colour[2], like a forest on fire for ever. He set out on his adventures across that coloured plain; and he has not come to the end of it yet.

Such is the story of Peter and Paul, which contains all the highest qualities of a modern fairy tale, including that of being wholly unfit for children; and indeed the motive with which I have introduced it is not childish, but rather full of subtlety and reaction. It is in fact the almost desperate motive of excusing or palliating the pages that follow. Peter and Paul are the two primary influences upon European literature to-day; and I may be permitted to put my own preference in its most favourable shape, even if I can only do it by what little girls call telling a story.

---

1. Honestly I don't know exactly what he means by Neo-Catholic Philosophy. It could mean something to do with Vatican I in 1870. It could be a movement following the French Revolution. I assume he's being somewhat silly and that what really matters is what the guy reads from his book in the next sentence. Don't let it trip you up.

2. British spellings. Deal with it.

I need scarcely say that I am the pigmy. The only excuse for the scraps that follow is that they show what can be achieved with a commonplace existence and the sacred spectacles of exaggeration. The other great literary theory, that which is roughly represented in England by Mr. Rudyard Kipling[3], is that we moderns are to regain the primal zest by sprawling all over the world growing used to travel and geographical variety, being at home everywhere, that is being at home nowhere.

Let it be granted that a man in a frock coat[4] is a heartrending sight; and the two alternative methods still remain. Mr. Kipling's school advises us to go to Central Africa in order to find a man without a frock coat. The school to which I belong suggests that we should stare steadily at the man until we see the man inside the frock coat. If we stare at him long enough he may even be moved to take off his coat to us; and that is a far greater compliment than his taking off his hat.

In other words, we may, by fixing our attention almost fiercely on the facts actually before us, force them to turn into adventures; force them to give up their meaning and fulfill their mysterious purpose. The purpose of the Kipling literature is to show how many extraordinary things a man may see if he is active and strides from continent to continent like the giant in my tale. But the object of my school is to show how many extraordinary things even a lazy and ordinary man may see if he can spur himself to the single activity of seeing.

For this purpose I have taken the laziest person of my acquaintance, that is myself; and made an idle diary of such odd things as I have fallen over by accident, in walking in a very limited area at a very indolent pace. If anyone says that these are very small affairs talked about in very big language, I can only gracefully compliment him upon seeing the joke. If anyone says that I am making mountains out of molehills, I confess with pride that it is so. I can imagine no more successful and productive form of manufacture than that of making mountains out of molehills. But I would add this not unimportant

---

3. The Jungle Book guy. More on him in later footnotes.

4. A fancy pants coat that hangs down to your knees.

fact, that molehills are mountains; one has only to become a pygmy like Peter to discover that.

I have my doubts about all this real value in mountaineering, in getting to the top of everything and overlooking everything. Satan was the most celebrated of Alpine guides, when he took Jesus to the top of an exceeding high mountain and showed him all the kingdoms of the earth. But the joy of Satan in standing on a peak is not a joy in largeness, but a joy in beholding smallness, in the fact that all men look like insects at his feet. It is from the valley that things look large; it is from the level that things look high; I am a child of the level and have no need of that celebrated Alpine guide. I will lift up my eyes to the hills, from whence cometh my help; but I will not lift up my carcass to the hills, unless it is absolutely necessary. Everything is in an attitude of mind; and at this moment I am in a comfortable attitude. I will sit still and let the marvels and the adventures settle on me like flies. There are plenty of them, I assure you. The world will never starve for want of wonders; but only for want of wonder.[5]

---

5. If that was the first Chesterton Essay you ever read, pat yourself on the back. You just jumped out of the "people who only know G.K. Chesterton quotes" club and into the super elite "people who actually have read G.K. Chesterton Club."

A Piece of Chalk

Tremendous Trifles **(1909)**

*"Chastity does not mean abstention from
sexual wrong; it means something
flaming, like Joan of Arc."*

IT IS POSSIBLE that my Chesterton obsession began when I realized he
was an illustrator—and not just an illustrator—a cartoonist (like me, for
readers who don't know that). In this sense, he speaks my language in a way
many authors do not. He went to school for art, and I believe dropped out.
He was just too good at writing to ever really launch an art career, I guess.

I love this essay because it is about making art, and it is very specific to
the concept of drawing on neutral colored paper (like brown) and pulling
out your highlights with white and filling in your shadows with black. It
is a much more dynamic way of adding dimension to your sketches than
simply drawing on white paper. But if you don't have white when drawing

on brown paper, it is completely pointless. A black and brown drawing is like a drawing in the dark.

A big Chesterton theme in this essay is that the world is good. It has gone bad because of fallen man, but the original creation is God's good work. Chesterton has many essays like this in *Tremendous Trifles*, where he depicts himself as this sort of wandering buffoon, stumbling on deep and meaningful truths after bumping into random things people usually pass right by.

I remember one splendid morning, all blue and silver, in the summer holidays when I reluctantly tore myself away from the task of doing nothing in particular, and put on a hat of some sort and picked up a walking-stick, and put six very bright-coloured chalks in my pocket. I then went into the kitchen (which, along with the rest of the house, belonged to a very square and sensible old woman in a Sussex village), and asked the owner and occupant of the kitchen if she had any brown paper. She had a great deal; in fact, she had too much; and she mistook the purpose and the rationale of the existence of brown paper. She seemed to have an idea that if a person wanted brown paper he must be wanting to tie up parcels; which was the last thing I wanted to do; indeed, it is a thing which I have found to be beyond my mental capacity. Hence she dwelt very much on the varying qualities of toughness and endurance in the material. I explained to her that I only wanted to draw pictures on it, and that I did not want them to endure in the least; and that from my point of view, therefore, it was a question, not of tough consistency, but of responsive surface, a thing comparatively irrelevant in a parcel. When she understood that I wanted to draw she offered to overwhelm me with note-paper, apparently supposing that I did my notes and correspondence on old brown paper wrappers from motives of economy.

I then tried to explain the rather delicate logical shade, that I not only liked brown paper, but liked the quality of brownness[1] in paper, just as I liked the

---

1. One thing that might not make sense if you have never gotten into sketching, especially using a full range of shades from white to black chalk or conte, is that brown paper works as a great neutral color, from it you can add black shadows and white highlights and the image produced has a lot more dimension to it than something drawn on plain white paper. (To show an example of this, I did the cover of this book in this style. See? That's just black, white, and brown paper, though admittedly I did it on my iPad, same effect.)

quality of brownness in October woods, or in beer, or in the peat-streams of the North. Brown paper represents the primal twilight of the first toil of creation, and with a bright-coloured chalk or two you can pick out points of fire in it, sparks of gold, and blood-red, and sea-green, like the first fierce stars that sprang out of divine darkness. All this I said (in an off-hand way) to the old woman; and I put the brown paper in my pocket along with the chalks, and possibly other things. I suppose every one must have reflected how primeval and how poetical are the things that one carries in one's pocket; the pocket-knife, for instance, the type of all human tools, the infant of the sword. Once I planned to write a book of poems entirely about the things in my pockets. But I found it would be too long; and the age of the great epics is past.

With my stick and my knife, my chalks and my brown paper, I went out on to the great downs[2]. I crawled across those colossal contours that express the best quality of England, because they are at the same time soft and strong. The smoothness of them has the same meaning as the smoothness of great cart-horses, or the smoothness of the beech-tree; it declares in the teeth of our timid and cruel theories that the mighty are merciful. As my eye swept the landscape, the landscape was as kindly as any of its cottages, but for power it was like an earthquake. The villages in the immense valley were safe, one could see, for centuries; yet the lifting of the whole land was like the lifting of one enormous wave to wash them all away.

I crossed one swell of living turf after another, looking for a place to sit down and draw. Do not, for heaven's sake, imagine I was going to sketch from Nature. I was going to draw devils and seraphim, and blind old gods that men worshipped before the dawn of right, and saints in robes of angry crimson, and seas of strange green, and all the sacred or monstrous symbols that look so well in bright colours on brown paper. They are much better worth drawing

---

2. Forgive me but I was never really clear on what "downs" were because I'm American. They are ridges of undulating chalk and limestone hills in southern England, with few trees and used mainly for pasture.

than Nature; also they are much easier to draw. When a cow came slouching by in the field next to me, a mere artist might have drawn it; but I always get wrong in the hind legs of quadrupeds. So I drew the soul of the cow; which I saw there plainly walking before me in the sunlight; and the soul was all purple and silver, and had seven horns and the mystery that belongs to all the beasts. But though I could not with a crayon get the best out of the landscape, it does not follow that the landscape was not getting the best out of me. And this, I think, is the mistake that people make about the old poets who lived before Wordsworth[3], and were supposed not to care very much about Nature because they did not describe it much.

They preferred writing about great men to writing about great hills; but they sat on the great hills to write it. They gave out much less about Nature, but they drank in, perhaps, much more. They painted the white robes of their holy virgins with the blinding snow, at which they had stared all day. They blazoned the shields of their paladins with the purple and gold of many heraldic sunsets. The greenness of a thousand green leaves clustered into the live green figure of Robin Hood. The blueness of a score of forgotten skies became the blue robes of the Virgin. The inspiration went in like sunbeams and came out like Apollo.[4]

But as I sat scrawling these silly figures on the brown paper, it began to dawn on me, to my great disgust, that I had left one chalk, and that a most exquisite and essential chalk, behind. I searched all my pockets, but I could not find any white chalk. Now, those who are acquainted with all the philosophy (nay, religion) which is typified in the art of drawing on brown paper, know that white is positive and essential. I cannot avoid remarking here upon a moral significance. One of the wise and awful truths which this brown-paper art reveals, is this, that white is a colour. It is not a mere absence of colour; it is a shining and affirmative thing, as fierce as red, as definite as black. When, so

---

3. Not sure if this helps but Wordsworth was a romantic poet and poet laureate of the United Kingdeom from 1843-1850 when he passed away.

4. Apollo: Olympian god of the sun and light.

to speak, your pencil grows red-hot, it draws roses; when it grows white-hot, it draws stars. And one of the two or three defiant verities of the best religious morality, of real Christianity, for example, is exactly this same thing; the chief assertion of religious morality is that white is a colour. Virtue is not the absence of vices or the avoidance of moral dangers; virtue is a vivid and separate thing, like pain or a particular smell. Mercy does not mean not being cruel or sparing people revenge or punishment; it means a plain and positive thing like the sun, which one has either seen or not seen.

Chastity does not mean abstention from sexual wrong; it means something flaming, like Joan of Arc[5]. In a word, God paints in many colours; but He never paints so gorgeously, I had almost said so gaudily, as when He paints in white. In a sense our age has realised this fact, and expressed it in our sullen costume. For if it were really true that white was a blank and colourless thing, negative and non-committal, then white would be used instead of black and grey for the funeral dress of this pessimistic period. We should see city gentlemen in frock coats of spotless silver linen, with top hats as white as wonderful arum lilies. Which is not the case.

Meanwhile, I could not find my chalk.

I sat on the hill in a sort of despair. There was no town nearer than Chichester at which it was even remotely probable that there would be such a thing as an artist's colourman. And yet, without white, my absurd little pictures would be as pointless as the world would be if there were no good people in it. I stared stupidly round, racking my brain for expedients. Then I suddenly stood up and roared with laughter, again and again, so that the cows stared at me and called a committee. Imagine a man in the Sahara regretting that he had no sand for his hour-glass. Imagine a gentleman in mid-ocean wishing that he had brought some salt water with him for his chemical experiments. I was sitting on an im-

5. Hero and saint of the Hundred Years War, the complete bad ass Joan of Arc was burned at the stake at age 19.

mense warehouse of white chalk. The landscape was made entirely out of white chalk. White chalk was piled more miles until it met the sky. I stooped and broke a piece off the rock I sat on; it did not mark so well as the shop chalks do; but it gave the effect. And I stood there in a trance of pleasure, realising that this Southern England is not only a grand peninsula, and a tradition and a civilisation; it is something even more admirable. It is a piece of chalk.

Introductory Remarks on the Importance of Orthodoxy

Heretics (1905)

"Everything matters—except everything."

ANOTHER INTRODUCTION! This was the introduction to Chesterton's book *Heretics*, which was a chapter-by-chapter take-down of the contemporary thinkers of his time. Modernists who were all going for efficiency and "art for art's sake." People had stopped caring about fundamental ideals, a philosophy of the Universe, meaning and eternity. They were only concerned with what worked. In the book, he takes on H.G. Wells, George Bernard Shaw, Rudyard Kipling and more.

I guess my tendency to share the introductory chapters of Chesterton's books can be blamed on the fact that these are the chapters where he doesn't get into the weeds too much. It's good to read these to get a sense of his ideas and where he is headed. It is much easier to understand where he is going once you grasp his bigger ideas.

And honestly, what really made me add this chapter is that last paragraph—one of my favorites.

NOTHING MORE STRANGELY indicates an enormous and silent evil of modern society than the extraordinary use which is made nowadays of the word "orthodox." In former days the heretic was proud of not being a heretic. It was the kingdoms of the world and the police and the judges who were heretics. He was orthodox. He had no pride in having rebelled against them; they had rebelled against him. The armies with their cruel security, the kings with their cold faces, the decorous processes of State, the reasonable processes of law—all these like sheep had gone astray. The man was proud of being orthodox, was proud of being right. If he stood alone in a howling wilderness he was more than a man; he was a church. He was the centre of the universe; it was round him that the stars swung. All the tortures torn out of forgotten hells could not make him admit that he was heretical. But a few modern phrases have made him boast of it. He says, with a conscious laugh, "I suppose I am very heretical," and looks round for applause.[1]

The word "heresy" not only means no longer being wrong; it practically means being clear-headed and courageous. The word "orthodoxy" not only no longer means being right; it practically means being wrong. All this can mean one thing, and one thing only. It means that people care less for whether they are philosophically right. For obviously a man ought to confess

1. This is such a perfect picture of this type of person. Sorry, not a real footnote. Carry on.

himself crazy before he confesses himself heretical. The Bohemian, with a red tie, ought to pique himself on his orthodoxy. The dynamiter, laying a bomb, ought to feel that, whatever else he is, at least he is orthodox.

It is foolish, generally speaking, for a philosopher to set fire to another philosopher in Smithfield Market[2] because they do not agree in their theory of the universe. That was done very frequently in the last decadence of the Middle Ages, and it failed altogether in its object. But there is one thing that is infinitely more absurd and unpractical than burning a man for his philosophy. This is the habit of saying that his philosophy does not matter, and this is done universally in the twentieth century, in the decadence of the great revolutionary period. General theories are everywhere contemned; the doctrine of the Rights of Man is dismissed with the doctrine of the Fall of Man. Atheism itself is too theological for us to-day. Revolution itself is too much of a system; liberty itself is too much of a restraint. We will have no generalizations. Mr. Bernard Shaw[3] has put the view in a perfect epigram: "The golden rule is that there is no golden rule." We are more and more to discuss details in art, politics, literature. A man's opinion on tramcars matters; his opinion on Botticelli[4] matters; his opinion on all things does not matter. He may turn over and explore a million objects, but he must not find that strange object, the universe; for if he does he will have a religion, and be lost. Everything matters—except everything.

Examples are scarcely needed of this total levity on the subject of cosmic philosophy. Examples are scarcely needed to show that, whatever else we think of as affecting practical affairs, we do not think it matters whether a man is a pessimist or an optimist, a Cartesian[5] or a Hegelian[6], a materialist

2. Many heretics were burned in Smithfield.

3. Shaw is mentioned many times in Chesterton's writings. They were good friends though they disagreed on nearly everything. Shaw was an atheist, and debates between Shaw and Chesterton were uproarious and full of playful jabs.

4. Botticelli: Italian painter who painted that famous image of the naked lady covering up her privates with her super long hair. (You know, she was on the cover of Adobe Illustrator for a long time).

5. Relating to Descartes and his ideas; Cartesianism is a form of rationalism because it holds that scientific knowledge can be derived a priori from 'innate ideas' through deductive reasoning, as opposed to empiricism, which puts it emphasis on sensory experience as the source of all knowledge.

6. The philosophy of G. W. F. Hegel which can be summed up by the dictum that "the rational alone is real", which means that all reality is capable of being expressed in rational categories. His goal was to reduce real-

or a spiritualist. Let me, however, take a random instance. At any innocent tea-table we may easily hear a man say, "Life is not worth living." We regard it as we regard the statement that it is a fine day; nobody thinks that it can possibly have any serious effect on the man or on the world. And yet if that utterance were really believed, the world would stand on its head. Murderers would be given medals for saving men from life; firemen would be denounced for keeping men from death; poisons would be used as medicines; doctors would be called in when people were well; the Royal Humane Society would be rooted out like a horde of assassins. Yet we never speculate as to whether the conversational pessimist will strengthen or disorganize society; for we are convinced that theories do not matter.

This was certainly not the idea of those who introduced our freedom. When the old Liberals removed the gags from all the heresies, their idea was that religious and philosophical discoveries might thus be made. Their view was that cosmic truth was so important that every one ought to bear inde-pendent testimony. The modern idea is that cosmic truth is so unimportant that it cannot matter what any one says. The former freed inquiry as men loose a noble hound; the latter frees inquiry as men fling back into the sea a fish unfit for eating.

Never has there been so little discussion about the nature of men as now, when, for the first time, any one can discuss it. The old restriction meant that only the orthodox were allowed to discuss religion. Modern liberty means that nobody is allowed to discuss it. Good taste, the last and vilest of human superstitions, has succeeded in silencing us where all the rest have failed. Sixty years ago it was bad taste to be an avowed atheist. Then came the Bradlaughites[7], the last religious men, the last men who cared about God; but they could not alter it. It is still bad taste to be an avowed atheist. But their agony has achieved just this—that now it is equally bad taste to be an avowed Christian. Emancipation has only locked the saint in the same tower of silence

ity to a more synthetic unity within the system of absolute idealism.

7. Charles Bradlaugh was an English political activist and atheist. He founded the National Secular Society in 1866. I guess Bradlaughites were people who thought he was really cool

as the heresiarch[8]. Then we talk about Lord Anglesey[9] and the weather, and call it the complete liberty of all the creeds.

But there are some people, nevertheless—and I am one of them—who think that the most practical and important thing about a man is still his view of the universe. We think that for a landlady considering a lodger, it is important to know his income, but still more important to know his philosophy. We think that for a general about to fight an enemy, it is important to know the enemy's numbers, but still more important to know the enemy's philosophy. We think the question is not whether the theory of the cosmos affects matters, but whether in the long run, anything else affects them. In the fifteenth century men cross-examined and tormented a man because he preached some immoral attitude; in the nineteenth century we feted and flattered Oscar Wilde[10] because he preached such an attitude, and then broke his heart in penal servitude because he carried it out. It may be a question which of the two methods was the more cruel; there can be no kind of question which was the more ludicrous. The age of the Inquisition has not at least the disgrace of having produced a society which made an idol of the very same man for preaching the very same things which it made him a convict for practising.

Now, in our time, philosophy or religion, our theory, that is, about ultimate things, has been driven out, more or less simultaneously, from two fields which it used to occupy. General ideals used to dominate literature. They have been driven out by the cry of "art for art's sake." General ideals used to dominate politics. They have been driven out by the cry of "efficiency," which may roughly be translated as "politics for politics' sake." Persistently for the last twenty years the ideals of order or liberty have dwindled in our books; the ambitions of wit and eloquence have dwindled in our parliaments. Litera-

---

8. The founder of a heresy or the leader of a heretical sect. Example: Kathleen Kennedy.

9. From my non-British understanding, Anglesey refers to a title, not a specific man. His main point here is that we talk about meaningless modern politics but we aren't supposed to talk about the eternal realities beneath them.

10. Irish poet and playwright. One of the most popular playwrights in London in the 1800's. He was convicted for gross indecency for consensual homosexual acts and imprisoned. He died an early death from meningitis at age 46.

ture has purposely become less political; politics have purposely become less literary. General theories of the relation of things have thus been extruded from both; and we are in a position to ask, "What have we gained or lost by this extrusion? Is literature better, is politics better, for having discarded the moralist and the philosopher?"

When everything about a people is for the time growing weak and ineffective, it begins to talk about efficiency. So it is that when a man's body is a wreck he begins, for the first time, to talk about health. Vigorous organisms talk not about their processes, but about their aims. There cannot be any better proof of the physical efficiency of a man than that he talks cheerfully of a journey to the end of the world. And there cannot be any better proof of the practical efficiency of a nation than that it talks constantly of a journey to the end of the world, a journey to the Judgment Day and the New Jerusalem. There can be no stronger sign of a coarse material health than the tendency to run after high and wild ideals; it is in the first exuberance of infancy that we cry for the moon.

None of the strong men in the strong ages would have understood what you meant by working for efficiency. Hildebrand[11] would have said that he was working not for efficiency, but for the Catholic Church. Danton[12] would have said that he was working not for efficiency, but for liberty, equality, and fraternity. Even if the ideal of such men were simply the ideal of kicking a man downstairs, they thought of the end like men, not of the process like paralytics. They did not say, "Efficiently elevating my right leg, using, you will notice, the muscles of the thigh and calf, which are in excellent order, I—" Their feeling was quite different. They were so filled with the beautiful vision of the man lying flat at the foot of the staircase that in that ecstasy the rest followed in a flash. In practice, the habit of generalizing and idealizing did not by any means mean worldly weakness. The time of big theories was the time of big results. In the era of sentiment and fine words, at the end of the

---

11. Not sure who is being referred to here. Best I can tell is it is a character from Germanic legend.

12. George Jacques Danton was a leading figure in the early stages of the French Revolution, in particular as the first president of the Committee of Public Safety.

eighteenth century, men were really robust and effective. The sentimentalists conquered Napoleon. The cynics could not catch De Wet[13].

A hundred years ago our affairs for good or evil were wielded triumphantly by rhetoricians. Now our affairs are hopelessly muddled by strong, silent men. And just as this repudiation of big words and big visions has brought forth a race of small men in politics, so it has brought forth a race of small men in the arts. Our modern politicians claim the colossal license of Caesar and the Superman, claim that they are too practical to be pure and too patriotic to be moral; but the upshot of it all is that a mediocrity is Chancellor of the Exchequer[14]. Our new artistic philosophers call for the same moral license, for a freedom to wreck heaven and earth with their energy; but the upshot of it all is that a mediocrity is Poet Laureate[15]. I do not say that there are no stronger men than these; but will any one say that there are any men stronger than those men of old who were dominated by their philosophy and steeped in their religion? Whether bondage be better than freedom may be discussed. But that their bondage came to more than our freedom it will be difficult for any one to deny.

The theory of the unmorality of art has established itself firmly in the strictly artistic classes. They are free to produce anything they like. They are free to write a "Paradise Lost" in which Satan shall conquer God. They are free to write a "Divine Comedy" in which heaven shall be under the floor of hell. And what have they done? Have they produced in their universality anything grander or more beautiful than the things uttered by the fierce Ghibbeline Catholic[16], by the rigid Puritan schoolmaster? We know that they

---

13. Christiaan Rudolf de Wet was a Boer war general, rebel leader and politician.

14. Sorry but I don't know England stuff so I have to Google it. The Chancellor of the Exchequer, often abbreviated to the Chancellor, is a high ranking Minister of the Crown within the Government of the United Kingdom, and head of Her Majesty's Treasury. As one of the four Great Offices of State, the chancellor is a senior member of the British Cabinet.

15. A poet officially appointed by a government or conferring institution, typically expected to compose poems for special events and occasions.

16. You can Google this if you need more context, but for the purposes of this portion of the chapter suffice it to say those Ghibbeline Catholics were real fighters. Glad I could help

have produced only a few roundels[17]. Milton[18] does not merely beat them at his piety, he beats them at their own irreverence. In all their little books of verse you will not find a finer defiance of God than Satan's. Nor will you find the grandeur of paganism felt as that fiery Christian felt it who described Faranata lifting his head as in disdain of hell. And the reason is very obvious. Blasphemy is an artistic effect, because blasphemy depends upon a philosophical conviction. Blasphemy depends upon belief and is fading with it. If any one doubts this, let him sit down seriously and try to think blasphemous thoughts about Thor. I think his family will find him at the end of the day in a state of some exhaustion.

Neither in the world of politics nor that of literature, then, has the rejection of general theories proved a success. It may be that there have been many moonstruck and misleading ideals that have from time to time perplexed mankind. But assuredly there has been no ideal in practice so moonstruck and misleading as the ideal of practicality. Nothing has lost so many opportunities as the opportunism of Lord Rosebery[19]. He is, indeed, a standing symbol of this epoch—the man who is theoretically a practical man, and practically more unpractical than any theorist. Nothing in this universe is so unwise as that kind of worship of worldly wisdom. A man who is perpetually thinking of whether this race or that race is strong, of whether this cause or that cause is promising, is the man who will never believe in anything long enough to make it succeed. The opportunist politician is like a man who should abandon billiards because he was beaten at billiards, and abandon golf because he was beaten at golf. There is nothing which is so weak for working purposes as this enormous importance attached to immediate victory. There is nothing that fails like success.

---

17. A small disc or decorated medallion.

18. You know, the Paradise Lost guy.

19. Archibald Philip Primrose, 5th Earl of Rosebery, 1st Earl of Midlothian, was Prime Minister of the United Kingdom from March 1894 to June 1895. Rosebery was widely known as a brilliant orator, an outstanding sportsman and marksman, a writer and historian, connoisseur and collector. All of these activities attracted him more than politics, which grew boring and unattractive. Historians judge him a failure as foreign minister and as prime minister.

And having discovered that opportunism does fail, I have been induced to look at it more largely, and in consequence to see that it must fail. I perceive that it is far more practical to begin at the beginning and discuss theories. I see that the men who killed each other about the orthodoxy of the Homoousion[20] were far more sensible than the people who are quarrelling about the Education Act. For the Christian dogmatists were trying to establish a reign of holiness, and trying to get defined, first of all, what was really holy. But our modern educationists are trying to bring about a religious liberty without attempting to settle what is religion or what is liberty. If the old priests forced a statement on mankind, at least they previously took some trouble to make it lucid. It has been left for the modern mobs of Anglicans and Nonconformists to persecute for a doctrine without even stating it.

For these reasons, and for many more, I for one have come to believe in going back to fundamentals. Such is the general idea of this book. I wish to deal with my most distinguished contemporaries, not personally or in a merely literary manner, but in relation to the real body of doctrine which they teach. I am not concerned with Mr. Rudyard Kipling[21] as a vivid artist or a vigorous personality; I am concerned with him as a Heretic—that is to say, a man whose view of things has the hardihood to differ from mine. I am not concerned with Mr. Bernard Shaw[22] as one of the most brilliant and one of the most honest men alive; I am concerned with him as a Heretic—that is to say, a man whose philosophy is quite solid, quite coherent, and quite wrong. I revert to the doctrinal methods of the thirteenth century, inspired by the general hope of getting something done.

Suppose[23] that a great commotion arises in the street about something, let us say a lamp-post, which many influential persons desire to pull down. A grey-clad monk, who is the spirit of the Middle Ages, is approached upon the

20. Homoousion is a Christian theological term, most notably used in the Nicene Creed for describing Jesus as "same in being" or "same in essence" with God the Father. The same term was later also applied to the Holy Spirit in order to designate him as being "same in essence" with the Father and the Son.

21. Chesterton took on Kipling in Heretics for his belief that by travelling the world he was experiencing humanity in a bigger way than someone from a small town.

22. More on Shaw in later footnotes, suffice it to say here Shaw and Chesterton disagreed on almost everything but were dear friends.

23. Yeah, here's the paragraph. Savor this!

matter, and begins to say, in the arid manner of the Schoolmen, "Let us first of all consider, my brethren, the value of Light. If Light be in itself good—" At this point he is somewhat excusably knocked down. All the people make a rush for the lamp-post, the lamp-post is down in ten minutes, and they go about congratulating each other on their unmediaeval practicality. But as things go on they do not work out so easily. Some people have pulled the lamp-post down because they wanted the electric light; some because they wanted old iron; some because they wanted darkness, because their deeds were evil. Some thought it not enough of a lamp-post, some too much; some acted because they wanted to smash municipal machinery; some because they wanted to smash something. And there is war in the night, no man knowing whom he strikes. So, gradually and inevitably, to-day, to-morrow, or the next day, there comes back the conviction that the monk was right after all, and that all depends on what is the philosophy of Light. Only what we might have discussed under the gas-lamp, we now must discuss in the dark.[24]

---

24. Read that paragraph again it's so good.

On Certain Modern Writers and the Institution of the Family

Heretics (**1905**)

"The best way that a man could test his readiness to encounter the common variety of mankind would be to climb down a chimney into any house at random, and get on as well as possible with the people inside. And that is essentially what each one of us did on the day that he was born."

THIS WAS ONE of the first Chesterton essays that really struck me. I was living in Portland, Oregon. I had recently moved up there from my small hometown of Coos Bay. I had made the move expecting a broader, bigger, wider experience. I made the mistake Chesterton cites in this chapter. He makes the point that you do not move to a big city to experience more of humanity, but less. In a city there is such a fierce variety of people, and such a large number, that it's possible to create such a customized and specific group of friends that you never really have to think outside of the bubble you have created. This is what people do in the name of being free-spirited and open-minded; they insulate into cliques. Then they define freedom as "being just like me and my highly-specific group."

I was taken back by how insular and narrow-minded many of the groups I tried to fit in with in Portland were. I could not be myself. It was great finally being somewhere I could hang out with other comic book artists, but when I got there I found a narrow club with very specific attitudes and politics.

I do think it is good to point out that, in this essay, Chesterton is not saying that the city is a bad thing, *per se*. He is simply saying not to lie to yourself and claim that you are going there to truly experience humanity or to broaden your view of mankind. Cities are designed to narrow us, and we all have a predisposition to seek to be narrow while appearing broad-minded.

THE FAMILY MAY fairly be considered, one would think, an ultimate human institution. Every one would admit that it has been the main cell and central unit of almost all societies hitherto, except, indeed, such societies as that of Lacedaemon[1], which went in for "efficiency," and has, therefore, perished, and left not a trace behind. Christianity, even enormous as was its revolution, did not alter this ancient and savage sanctity; it merely reversed it. It did not deny the trinity of father, mother, and child. It merely read it backwards, making it run child, mother, father. This it called, not the family, but the Holy Family, for many things are made holy by being turned upside down. But some sages of our own decadence have made a serious attack on the family. They have impugned it, as I think wrongly; and its defenders have defended it, and defended it wrongly. The common defence of the family is that, amid the stress and fickleness of life, it is peaceful, pleasant, and at one. But there is another defence of the family which is possible, and to me evident; this defence is that the family is not peaceful and not pleasant and not at one.

It is not fashionable to say much nowadays of the advantages of the small community. We are told that we must go in for large empires and large ideas.

---

1. AKA Sparta, which, if you have ever seen 300 you saw how they treated kids, gees. Not good. Oh I guess if you didn't see it, they tossed out the weak ones like garbage and made them fight wolves and stuff. Well, according to the historically accurate Zack Snyder movie anyway.

There is one advantage, however, in the small state, the city, or the village, which only the wilfully blind can overlook. The man who lives in a small community lives in a much larger world. He knows much more of the fierce varieties and uncompromising divergences of men. The reason is obvious. In a large community we can choose our companions. In a small community our companions are chosen for us.

Thus in all extensive and highly civilized societies groups come into existence founded upon what is called sympathy, and shut out the real world more sharply than the gates of a monastery. There is nothing really narrow about the clan; the thing which is really narrow is the clique. The men of the clan live together because they all wear the same tartan or are all descended from the same sacred cow; but in their souls, by the divine luck of things, there will always be more colours than in any tartan. But the men of the clique live together because they have the same kind of soul, and their narrowness is a narrowness of spiritual coherence and contentment, like that which exists in hell. A big society exists in order to form cliques. A big society is a society for the promotion of narrowness. It is a machinery for the purpose of guarding the solitary and sensitive individual from all experience of the bitter and bracing human compromises. It is, in the most literal sense of the words, a society for the prevention of Christian knowledge.

We can see this change, for instance, in the modern transformation of the thing called a club. When London was smaller, and the parts of London more self-contained and parochial, the club was what it still is in villages, the opposite of what it is now in great cities. Then the club was valued as a place where a man could be sociable. Now the club is valued as a place where a man can be unsociable. The more the enlargement and elaboration of our civilization goes on the more the club ceases to be a place where a man can have a noisy argument, and becomes more and more a place where a man can have what is somewhat fantastically called a quiet chop. Its aim is to make a man comfortable, and to make a man comfortable is to make him the opposite of sociable. Sociability, like all good things, is full of discomforts, dangers, and renunciations. The club tends to produce the most degraded of all combinations—the luxurious anchorite, the man who combines the self-indulgence of Lucullus[2] with the insane loneliness of St. Simeon Stylites[3]. If we were to-morrow morning snowed up in the street in which we live, we should step suddenly into a much larger and much wilder world than we have ever known. And it is the whole effort of the typically modern person to escape from the street in which he lives. First he invents modern hygiene and goes to Margate[4]. Then he invents modern culture and goes to Florence. Then he invents modern imperialism and goes to Timbuctoo. He goes to the fantastic borders of the earth. He pretends to shoot tigers. He almost rides on a camel. And in all this he is still essentially fleeing from the street in which he was born; and of this flight he is always ready with his own explanation.

He says he is fleeing from his street because it is dull; he is lying. He is really fleeing from his street because it is a great deal too exciting. It is exciting because it is exacting; it is exacting because it is alive. He can visit Venice because to him the Venetians are only Venetians; the people in his own street are men. He can stare at the Chinese because for him the Chinese are a passive thing to be stared at; if he stares at the old lady in the next garden, she becomes active. He is forced to flee, in short, from the too stimulating society of his equals—of free men, perverse, personal, deliberately different from himself. The street in Brixton is too glowing and overpowering.

He has to soothe and quiet himself among tigers and vultures, camels and crocodiles. These creatures are indeed very different from himself. But they do not put their shape or colour or custom into a decisive intellectual

2. Lucius Licinius Lucullus (his parents were really into alliteration) was an "optimatis" (aristocrat) politician of the late Roman Republic, In the culmination of over twenty years of almost continuous military and government service, he became the conqueror of the Eastern Kingdoms in the course of the Third Mithridatic War. He returned with so much captured booty that the vast sums of treasure, jewels, priceless works of art, and slaves could not be fully accounted for. He poured enormous sums into private building projects, husbandry and even aquaculture projects which shocked and amazed his contemporaries by their magnitude.

3 A Syrian ascetic saint who achieved notability for living 37 years on a small platform on top of a pillar near Aleppo (in modern Syria) ...but where did he poo?!

4. In the UK... this may have some relation: In the late 18th century, the town was chosen by the physician John Coakley Lettsom as the place in which he would build the Royal Sea Bathing Hospital, which was the first of its kind in Britain.

competition with his own. They do not seek to destroy his principles and assert their own; the stranger monsters of the suburban street do seek to do this. The camel does not contort his features into a fine sneer because Mr. Robinson has not got a hump; the cultured gentleman at No. 5 does exhibit a sneer because Robinson has not got a dado[5]. The vulture will not roar with laughter because a man does not fly; but the major at No. 9 will roar with laughter because a man does not smoke.

The complaint we commonly have to make of our neighbours is that they will not, as we express it, mind their own business. We do not really mean that they will not mind their own business. If our neighbours did not mind their own business they would be asked abruptly for their rent, and would rapidly cease to be our neighbours. What we really mean when we say that they cannot mind their own business is something much deeper. We do not dislike them because they have so little force and fire that they cannot be interested in themselves. We dislike them because they have so much force and fire that they can be interested in us as well. What we dread about our neighbours, in short, is not the narrowness of their horizon, but their superb tendency to broaden it. And all aversions to ordinary humanity have this general character. They are not aversions to its feebleness (as is pretended), but to its energy. The misanthropes pretend that they despise humanity for its weakness. As a matter of fact, they hate it for its strength.

Of course, this shrinking from the brutal vivacity and brutal variety of common men is a perfectly reasonable and excusable thing as long as it does not pretend to any point of superiority. It is when it calls itself aristocracy or aestheticism or a superiority to the bourgeoisie that its inherent weakness has in justice to be pointed out. Fastidiousness is the most pardonable of vices; but it is the most unpardonable of virtues. Nietzsche, who represents most prominently this pretentious claim of the fastidious, has a description somewhere—a very powerful description in the purely literary sense—of the disgust and disdain which consume him at the sight of the common people

---

5. The lower part of the wall of a room, below about waist height, if it is a different color or has a different covering than the upper part. So, the gentleman at number 5 is very particular about interior decoration, I guess?

with their common faces, their common voices, and their common minds. As I have said, this attitude is almost beautiful if we may regard it as pathetic. Nietzsche's aristocracy has about it all the sacredness that belongs to the weak. When he makes us feel that he cannot endure the innumerable faces, the incessant voices, the overpowering omnipresence which belongs to the mob, he will have the sympathy of anybody who has ever been sick on a steamer or tired in a crowded omnibus. Every man has hated mankind when he was less than a man. Every man has had humanity in his eyes like a blinding fog, humanity in his nostrils like a suffocating smell. But when Nietzsche has the incredible lack of humour and lack of imagination to ask us to believe that his aristocracy is an aristocracy of strong muscles or an aristocracy of strong wills, it is necessary to point out the truth. It is an aristocracy of weak nerves.

We make our friends; we make our enemies; but God makes our next-door neighbour. Hence he comes to us clad in all the careless terrors of nature; he is as strange as the stars, as reckless and indifferent as the rain. He is Man, the most terrible of the beasts. That is why the old religions and the old scriptural language showed so sharp a wisdom when they spoke, not of one's duty towards humanity, but one's duty towards one's neighbour. The duty towards humanity may often take the form of some choice which is personal or even pleasurable. That duty may be a hobby; it may even be a dissipation. We may work in the East End because we are peculiarly fitted to work in the East End, or because we think we are; we may fight for the cause of international peace because we are very fond of fighting. The most monstrous martyrdom, the most repulsive experience, may be the result of choice or a kind of taste. We may be so made as to be particularly fond of lunatics or specially interested in leprosy. We may love negroes because they are black or German Socialists because they are pedantic. But we have to love our neighbour because he is there—a much more alarming reason for a much more serious operation. He is the sample of humanity which is actually given us. Precisely because he may be anybody he is everybody. He is a symbol because he is an accident.

Doubtless men flee from small environments into lands that are very deadly. But this is natural enough; for they are not fleeing from death. They are fleeing from life. And this principle applies to ring within ring of the social system of humanity. It is perfectly reasonable that men should seek for some particular variety of the human type, so long as they are seeking for that variety of the human type, and not for mere human variety. It is quite proper that a British diplomatist should seek the society of Japanese generals, if what he wants is Japanese generals. But if what he wants is people different from himself, he had much better stop at home and discuss religion with the housemaid. It is quite reasonable that the village genius should come up to conquer London if what he wants is to conquer London. But if he wants to conquer something fundamentally and symbolically hostile and also very strong, he had much better remain where he is and have a row with the rector. The man in the suburban street is quite right if he goes to Ramsgate[6] for the sake of Ramsgate—a difficult thing to imagine. But if, as he expresses it, he goes to Ramsgate "for a change," then he would have a much more romantic and even melodramatic change if he jumped over the wall into his neighbours garden. The consequences would be bracing in a sense far beyond the possibilities of Ramsgate hygiene.

Now, exactly as this principle applies to the empire, to the nation within the empire, to the city within the nation, to the street within the city, so it applies to the home within the street. The institution of the family is to be commended for precisely the same reasons that the institution of the nation, or the institution of the city, are in this matter to be commended. It is a good thing for a man to live in a family for the same reason that it is a good thing for a man to be besieged in a city. It is a good thing for a man to live in a family in the same sense that it is a beautiful and delightful thing for a man to be snowed up in a street. They all force him to realize that life is not a thing from outside, but a thing from inside. Above all, they all insist upon the fact that life, if it be a truly stimulating and fascinating life, is a thing which, of its nature, exists in spite of ourselves.

---

6. Ramsgate is a seaside town in the district of Thanet in east Kent, England. It was one of the great English seaside towns of the 19th century.

The modern writers who have suggested, in a more or less open manner, that the family is a bad institution, have generally confined themselves to suggesting, with much sharpness, bitterness, or pathos, that perhaps the family is not always very congenial. Of course the family is a good institution because it is uncongenial. It is wholesome precisely because it contains so many divergencies and varieties. It is, as the sentimentalists say, like a little kingdom, and, like most other little kingdoms, is generally in a state of something resembling anarchy. It is exactly because our brother George is not interested in our religious difficulties, but is interested in the Trocadero[7] Restaurant, that the family has some of the bracing qualities of the commonwealth. It is precisely because our uncle Henry does not approve of the theatrical ambitions of our sister Sarah that the family is like humanity. The men and women who, for good reasons and bad, revolt against the family, are, for good reasons and bad, simply revolting against mankind. Aunt Elizabeth is unreasonable, like mankind. Papa is excitable, like mankind. Our youngest brother is mischievous, like mankind. Grandpapa is stupid, like the world; he is old, like the world.

Those who wish, rightly or wrongly, to step out of all this, do definitely wish to step into a narrower world. They are dismayed and terrified by the largeness and variety of the family. Sarah wishes to find a world wholly consisting of private theatricals; George wishes to think the Trocadero a cosmos. I do not say, for a moment, that the flight to this narrower life may not be the right thing for the individual, any more than I say the same thing about flight into a monastery. But I do say that anything is bad and artificial which tends to make these people succumb to the strange delusion that they are stepping into a world which is actually larger and more varied than their own. The best way that a man could test his readiness to encounter the common variety of mankind would be to climb down a chimney into any house at random, and get on as well as possible with the people inside. And that is essentially what each one of us did on the day that he was born.

---

7. OK I honestly couldn't really find anything explaining to me what a Trocadero restaurant is. I found a few but no explanation as to what they serve. I guess it doesn't really matter. It's a restaurant. We get it. Moving on.

This is, indeed, the sublime and special romance of the family. It is romantic because it is a toss-up. It is romantic because it is everything that its enemies call it. It is romantic because it is arbitrary. It is romantic because it is there. So long as you have groups of men chosen rationally, you have some special or sectarian atmosphere. It is when you have groups of men chosen irrationally that you have men. The element of adventure begins to exist; for an adventure is, by its nature, a thing that comes to us. It is a thing that chooses us, not a thing that we choose.

Falling in love has been often regarded as the supreme adventure, the supreme romantic accident. In so much as there is in it something outside ourselves, something of a sort of merry fatalism, this is very true. Love does take us and transfigure and torture us. It does break our hearts with an unbearable beauty, like the unbearable beauty of music. But in so far as we have certainly something to do with the matter; in so far as we are in some sense prepared to fall in love and in some sense jump into it; in so far as we do to some extent choose and to some extent even judge—in all this falling in love is not truly romantic, is not truly adventurous at all. In this degree the supreme adventure is not falling in love. The supreme adventure is being born. There we do walk suddenly into a splendid and startling trap. There we do see something of which we have not dreamed before. Our father and mother do lie in wait for us and leap out on us, like brigands from a bush. Our uncle is a surprise. Our aunt is, in the beautiful common expression, a bolt from the blue. When we step into the family, by the act of being born, we do step into a world which is incalculable, into a world which has its own strange laws, into a world which could do without us, into a world that we have not made. In other words, when we step into the family we step into a fairy-tale.

This colour as of a fantastic narrative ought to cling to the family and to our relations with it throughout life. Romance is the deepest thing in life; romance is deeper even than reality. For even if reality could be proved to be misleading, it still could not be proved to be unimportant or unimpressive. Even if the facts are false, they are still very strange. And this strangeness of life, this unexpected and even perverse element of things as they fall out, remains incurably interesting. The circumstances we can regulate may become tame or pessimistic; but the "circumstances over which we have no control" remain god-like to those who, like Mr. Micawber[8], can call on them and renew their strength.

People wonder why the novel is the most popular form of literature; people wonder why it is read more than books of science or books of metaphysics. The reason is very simple; it is merely that the novel is more true than they are. Life may sometimes legitimately appear as a book of science. Life may sometimes appear, and with a much greater legitimacy, as a book of metaphysics. But life is always a novel. Our existence may cease to be a song; it may cease even to be a beautiful lament. Our existence may not be an intelligible justice, or even a recognizable wrong. But our existence is still a story. In the fiery alphabet of every sunset is written, "to be continued in our next."

If we have sufficient intellect, we can finish a philosophical and exact deduction, and be certain that we are finishing it right. With the adequate brain-power we could finish any scientific discovery, and be certain that we were finishing it right. But not with the most gigantic intellect could we finish the simplest or silliest story, and be certain that we were finishing it right. That is because a story has behind it, not merely intellect which is partly mechanical, but will, which is in its essence divine. The narrative writer can send his hero to the gallows if he likes in the last chapter but one. He can do it by the same divine caprice whereby he, the author, can go to the gallows himself, and to hell afterwards if he chooses. And the same civilization, the chivalric European civilization which asserted freewill in the thirteenth century, produced the thing called "fiction" in the eighteenth. When Thomas Aquinas asserted the spiritual liberty of man, he created all the bad novels in the circulating libraries.

But in order that life should be a story or romance to us, it is necessary that a great part of it, at any rate, should be settled for us without our permission. If we wish life to be a system, this may be a nuisance; but if we wish it to be

---

8. Wilkins Micawber is a clerk in Charles Dickens's 1850 novel David Copperfield. He is traditionally identified with the optimistic belief that "something will turn up."

a drama, it is an essential. It may often happen, no doubt, that a drama may be written by somebody else which we like very little. But we should like it still less if the author came before the curtain every hour or so, and forced on us the whole trouble of inventing the next act. A man has control over many things in his life; he has control over enough things to be the hero of a novel. But if he had control over everything, there would be so much hero that there would be no novel. And the reason why the lives of the rich are at bottom so tame and uneventful is simply that they can choose the events. They are dull because they are omnipotent. They fail to feel adventures because they can make the adventures.

The thing which keeps life romantic and full of fiery possibilities is the existence of these great plain limitations which force all of us to meet the things we do not like or do not expect. It is vain for the supercilious moderns to talk of being in uncongenial surroundings. To be in a romance is to be in uncongenial surroundings. To be born into this earth is to be born into un-congenial surroundings, hence to be born into a romance. Of all these great limitations and frameworks which fashion and create the poetry and variety of life, the family is the most definite and important. Hence it is misunder-stood by the moderns, who imagine that romance would exist most perfectly in a complete state of what they call liberty. They think that if a man makes a gesture it would be a startling and romantic matter that the sun should fall from the sky. But the startling and romantic thing about the sun is that it does not fall from the sky. They are seeking under every shape and form a world where there are no limitations—that is, a world where there are no outlines; that is, a world where there are no shapes. There is nothing baser than that infinity. They say they wish to be as strong as the universe, but they really wish the whole universe as weak as themselves.

On Lying In Bed

Tremendous Trifles **(1909)**

"If there is one thing worse than the modern weakening of major morals, it is the modern strengthening of minor morals."

ANOTHER ESSAY FROM *Tremendous Trifles*, this is similar in some ways to A Piece of Chalk. To be honest, what I really love about this essay is the visual I get when I imagine Chesterton lying in bed madly painting the ceiling with two brooms as paint drips all over his face.

But at the heart of this essay Chesterton is lamenting his culture's exalting of meaningless and small virtues like politeness, cleanliness, and getting up early, while tossing aside the deep eternal virtues of truth, goodness, and beauty. An example he gives is the "Ibsenite" who says drinking beer is bad but taking "Prussic acid" (cyanide) is OK—health is everything but life itself is nothing. His culture, much like ours, has a lot to say about how one must live life, but is silent on why life should be lived at all.

LYING IN BED would be an altogether perfect and supreme experience if only one had a coloured pencil long enough to draw on the ceiling. This, however, is not generally a part of the domestic apparatus on the premises. I think myself that the thing might be managed with several pails of Aspinall[1] and a broom. Only if one worked in a really sweeping and masterly way, and laid on the colour in great washes, it might drip down again on one's face in floods of rich and mingled colour like some strange fairy rain; and that would have its disadvantages. I am afraid it would be necessary to stick to black and white in this form of artistic composition. To that purpose, indeed, the white ceiling would be of the greatest possible use; in fact, it is the only use I think of a white ceiling being put to.

But for the beautiful experiment of lying in bed I might never have discovered it. For years I have been looking for some blank spaces in a modern house to draw on. Paper is much too small for any really allegorical design; as Cyrano de Bergerac says, "Il me faut des géants."[2] But when I tried to find these fine clear spaces in the modern rooms such as we all live in I was continually disappointed. I found an endless pattern and complication of small objects hung like a curtain of fine links between me and my desire. I examined the walls; I found them to my surprise to be already covered with wallpaper, and I found the wallpaper to be already covered with uninteresting images, all bearing a ridiculous resemblance to each other. I could not understand why one arbitrary symbol (a symbol apparently entirely devoid of any religious or philosophical significance) should thus be sprinkled all over my nice walls like a sort of small-pox[3]. The Bible must be referring to wallpapers, I think, when it says, "Use not vain repetitions, as the Gentiles do." I found the Turkey carpet a mass of unmeaning colours, rather like the Turkish Empire, or like

---

1. Aspinall was a brand of house paint in the 1800's.

2. From the play Cyrano de Bergerac, at Cyrano's highest moment he says:

> "I-I am going to be a storm-a flame-
> I need to fight whole armies alone;
> I have ten hearts; I have a hundred arms;
> I feel too strong to war with mortals- BRING ME GIANTS!"

That last part is what Chesterton quotes here in needing something bigger than mere paper to sketch on.

3. Boom. Wallpaper roasted.

the sweetmeat called Turkish Delight. I do not exactly know what Turkish Delight really is; but I suppose it is Macedonian Massacres[4]. Everywhere that I went forlornly, with my pencil or my paint brush, I found that others had unaccountably been before me, spoiling the walls, the curtains, and the furniture with their childish and barbaric designs.

Nowhere did I find a really clear space for sketching until this occasion when I prolonged beyond the proper limit the process of lying on my back in bed. Then the light of that white heaven broke upon my vision, that breadth of mere white which is indeed almost the definition of Paradise, since it means purity and also means freedom. But alas! like all heavens, now that it is seen it is found to be unattainable; it looks more austere and more distant than the blue sky outside the window. For my proposal to paint on it with the bristly end of a broom has been discouraged—never mind by whom; by a person debarred from all political rights—and even my minor proposal to put the other end of the broom into the kitchen fire and turn it to charcoal has not been conceded. Yet I am certain that it was from persons in my position that all the original inspiration came for covering the ceilings of palaces and cathedrals with a riot of fallen angels or victorious gods. I am sure that it was only because Michael Angelo was engaged in the ancient and honourable occupation of lying in bed that he ever realized how the roof of the Sistine Chapel might be made into an awful imitation of a divine drama that could only be acted in the heavens.

The tone now commonly taken toward the practice of lying in bed is hypocritical and unhealthy. Of all the marks of modernity that seem to mean a kind of decadence, there is none more menacing and dangerous than the exultation of very small and secondary matters of conduct at the expense of very great and primary ones, at the expense of eternal ties and tragic human

---

4. The Macedonian massacres of 1900 in which Turks were wiping out Christians. That's one macabre candy joke, GK.

morality. If there is one thing worse than the modern weakening of major morals, it is the modern strengthening of minor morals. Thus it is considered more withering to accuse a man of bad taste than of bad ethics. Cleanliness is not next to godliness nowadays, for cleanliness is made essential and godliness is regarded as an offence. A playwright can attack the institution of marriage so long as he does not misrepresent the manners of society, and I have met Ibsenite[5] pessimists who thought it wrong to take beer but right to take prussic acid[6]. Especially this is so in matters of hygiene; notably such matters as lying in bed. Instead of being regarded, as it ought to be, as a matter of personal convenience and adjustment, it has come to be regarded by many as if it were a part of essential morals to get up early in the morning. It is upon the whole part of practical wisdom; but there is nothing good about it or bad about its opposite.

Misers get up early in the morning; and burglars, I am informed, get up the night before. It is the great peril of our society that all its mechanisms may grow more fixed while its spirit grows more fickle. A man's minor actions and arrangements ought to be free, flexible, creative; the things that should be unchangeable are his principles, his ideals. But with us the reverse is true; our views change constantly; but our lunch does not change. Now, I should like men to have strong and rooted conceptions, but as for their lunch, let them have it sometimes in the garden, sometimes in bed, sometimes on the roof, sometimes in the top of a tree. Let them argue from the same first principles, but let them do it in a bed, or a boat, or a balloon. This alarming growth of good habits really means a too great emphasis on those virtues which mere custom can ensure, it means too little emphasis on those virtues which cus-

5. Ibsen was a Norwegian playwrite, considered one of the founders of "modernism in theater" and the "father of realism" - two things Chesterton would not be a fan of. He brings up Ibsen quite often in his writing. An Ibsenite, then, must be someone who thinks Ibsen is a really cool guy.

6. AKA cyanide.

tom can never quite ensure, sudden and splendid virtues of inspired pity or of inspired candour. If ever that abrupt appeal is made to us we may fail. A man can get use to getting up at five o'clock in the morning. A man cannot very well get used to being burnt for his opinions; the first experiment is commonly fatal. Let us pay a little more attention to these possibilities of the heroic and unexpected. I dare say that when I get out of this bed I shall do some deed of an almost terrible virtue.

For those who study the great art of lying in bed there is one emphatic caution to be added. Even for those who can do their work in bed (like journalists), still more for those whose work cannot be done in bed (as, for example, the professional harpooners of whales), it is obvious that the indulgence must be very occasional. But that is not the caution I mean. The caution is this: if you do lie in bed, be sure you do it without any reason or justification at all. I do not speak, of course, of the seriously sick. But if a healthy man lies in bed, let him do it without a rag of excuse; then he will get up a healthy man. If he does it for some secondary hygienic reason, if he has some scientific explanation, he may get up a hypochondriac.

On Running After One's Hat

All Things Considered (1915)

"An adventure is only an inconvenience rightly considered. An inconvenience is only an adventure wrongly considered."

THIS ESSAY HAS become a favorite among my coworkers at *The Babylon Bee*. We often reference it when things go wrong. It's all about perspective. When things don't go your way, especially when you might be having a particularly clumsy, blundering day, Chesterton says we should be proud of the fact that we are bringing the rest of the world so much joy in the moments we look the most foolish.

But the point is even deeper than that. We want to control life and have all of its contingencies figured out and prepared for. We want life to be comfortable and arranged and predictable. Life is not that, and thank God it is not, for if it were, there would be no adventure, no romance, and nothing truly hilarious.

Of course, it's not easy to adopt this attitude when your three-year-old has clogged the toilet for the 20th time or your car is billowing smoke on the side of the freeway. But if we can think of it as a comedy and the joy it brings us to laugh, maybe if we can look at our situation from outside, we might find our story a little more entertaining. In fact, I think it's true that many of our blunders are blessings even though we rarely can see it in the moment.

Maybe this essay will stick with you like it has me. Every time I am frustrated and feeling like everything is going wrong, I think of the phrase "running after one's hat."

I FEEL AN ALMOST savage envy on hearing that London has been flooded in my absence, while I am in the mere country. My own Battersea[1] has been, I understand, particularly favoured as a meeting of the waters. Battersea was already, as I need hardly say, the most beautiful of human localities. Now that it has the additional splendour of great sheets of water, there must be something quite incomparable in the landscape (or waterscape) of my own romantic town. Battersea must be a vision of Venice. The boat that brought the meat from the butcher's must have shot along those lanes of rippling silver with the strange smoothness of the gondola. The greengrocer who brought cabbages to the corner of the Latchmere Road[2] must have leant upon the oar with the unearthly grace of the gondolier. There is nothing so perfectly poetical as an island; and when a district is flooded it becomes an archipelago.

Some consider such romantic views of flood or fire slightly lacking in reality. But really this romantic view of such inconveniences is quite as practical as the other. The true optimist who sees in such things an opportunity for enjoyment is quite as logical and much more sensible than the ordinary "Indignant Ratepayer" who sees in them an opportunity for grumbling. Real pain, as in the case of being burnt at Smithfield or having a toothache, is a positive thing; it can be supported, but scarcely enjoyed. But, after all, our toothaches are the exception, and as for being burnt at Smithfield[3], it only happens to us at the very longest intervals. And most of the inconveniences

---

1. A part of London on the south bank of the River Thames.

2. A road in the Battersea area, if that's not obvious.

3. Many Christian martyrs were burned at Smithfield.

that make men swear or women cry are really sentimental or imaginative inconveniences—things altogether of the mind. For instance, we often hear grown-up people complaining of having to hang about a railway station and wait for a train. Did you ever hear a small boy complain of having to hang about a railway station and wait for a train? No; for to him to be inside a railway station is to be inside a cavern of wonder and a palace of poetical pleasures. Because to him the red light and the green light on the signal are like a new sun and a new moon. Because to him when the wooden arm of the signal falls down suddenly, it is as if a great king had thrown down his staff as a signal and started a shrieking tournament of trains. I myself am of little boys' habit in this matter. They also serve who only stand and wait for the two fifteen. Their meditations may be full of rich and fruitful things. Many of the most purple hours of my life have been passed at Clapham Junction[4], which is now, I suppose, under water. I have been there in many moods so fixed and mystical that the water might well have come up to my waist before I noticed it particularly. But in the case of all such annoyances, as I have said, everything depends upon the emotional point of view. You can safely apply the test to almost every one of the things that are currently talked of as the typical nuisance of daily life.

For instance, there is a current impression that it is unpleasant to have to run after one's hat. Why should it be unpleasant to the well-ordered and pious mind? Not merely because it is running, and running exhausts one. The same people run much faster in games and sports. The same people run much more eagerly after an uninteresting little leather ball than they will after a nice silk hat. There is an idea that it is humiliating to run after one's hat; and when people say it is humiliating they mean that it is comic. It certainly is comic; but man is a very comic creature, and most of the things he does are comic—eating, for instance. And the most comic things of all are exactly the things that are most worth doing—such as making love. A man running after a hat is not half so ridiculous as a man running after a wife.

4. A major railway station and transport hub near St John's Hill in south-west Battersea in the London Borough of Wandsworth.

Now a man could, if he felt rightly in the matter, run after his hat with the manliest ardour and the most sacred joy. He might regard himself as a jolly huntsman pursuing a wild animal, for certainly no animal could be wilder. In fact, I am inclined to believe that hat-hunting on windy days will be the sport of the upper classes in the future. There will be a meet of ladies and gentlemen on some high ground on a gusty morning. They will be told that the professional attendants have started a hat in such-and-such a thicket, or whatever be the technical term. Notice that this employment will in the fullest degree combine sport with humanitarianism. The hunters would feel that they were not inflicting pain. Nay, they would feel that they were inflicting pleasure, rich, almost riotous pleasure, upon the people who were looking on. When last I saw an old gentleman running after his hat in Hyde Park, I told him that a heart so benevolent as his ought to be filled with peace and thanks at the thought of how much unaffected pleasure his every gesture and bodily attitude were at that moment giving to the crowd.

The same principle can be applied to every other typical domestic worry. A gentleman trying to get a fly out of the milk or a piece of cork out of his glass of wine often imagines himself to be irritated. Let him think for a moment of the patience of anglers sitting by dark pools, and let his soul be immediately irradiated with gratification and repose. Again, I have known some people of very modern views driven by their distress to the use of theological terms to which they attached no doctrinal significance, merely because a drawer was jammed tight and they could not pull it out. A friend of mine was particularly afflicted in this way. Every day his drawer was jammed, and every day in consequence it was something else that rhymes to it. But I pointed out to him that this sense of wrong was really subjective and relative; it rested entirely upon the assumption that the drawer could, should, and would come out easily. "But if," I said, "you picture to yourself that you are pulling against some powerful and oppressive enemy, the struggle will become merely exciting and not exasperating. Imagine that you are tugging up a lifeboat out of the sea. Imagine that you are roping up a fellow-creature out of an Alpine crevass. Imagine even that you are a boy again and engaged in a tug-of-war between French and English." Shortly after saying this I left him; but I have no doubt at all that my words bore the best possible fruit. I have no doubt that every day of his life he hangs on to the handle of that drawer with a flushed face and eyes bright with battle, uttering encouraging shouts to himself, and seeming to hear all round him the roar of an applauding ring.

So I do not think that it is altogether fanciful or incredible to suppose that even the floods in London may be accepted and enjoyed poetically. Nothing beyond inconvenience seems really to have been caused by them; and inconvenience, as I have said, is only one aspect, and that the most un-imaginative and accidental aspect of a really romantic situation. An adventure is only an inconvenience rightly considered. An inconvenience is only an adventure wrongly considered. The water that girdled the houses and shops of London must, if anything, have only increased their previous witchery and wonder. For as the Roman Catholic priest in the story said: "Wine is good with everything except water," and on a similar principle, water is good with everything except wine.

Cheese

Alarms and Discursions (1910)

"Poets have been mysteriously silent on the subject of cheese."

THIS ESSAY IS best read aloud in a very dramatic, Shakespearean tone. Chesterton is often whimsical and conversational, but on the topic of bread and cheese he has the passion of Sir William Wallace on the edge of battle.

In this essay Chesterton is lamenting how modern society, as it takes over everything, stamps out the uniqueness, the soul of everything. In fact, it is hard 110 years later to even relate to what he is saying here about cheese. It seems in his time, if you went to a small town or village, each had its own local cheese which possessed its own character and qualities, with fresh baked bread that was equally exclusive to its locale. But when you went to the bigger cities they had the same cheeses shipped in from the big cheese factories and they didn't serve it with bread, but crackers (he calls them biscuits, lol). He compares this to soap, which—at the time—the same few brands were ubiquitous.

We have a lot of convenience now, but it's a trade-off. To find the soul of your fellow humans, to taste the essence of a small town, you have to seek it, because modernity is always trying to smudge it out, smooth out all the bumps and make everything into something shiny, safe, and highly manufactured. Someday, everything will just look like it was designed by Apple, all the way down to the food we eat, and I'm sure the iFoodPod will be very healthy, but I am even more sure that it will also be as vapid and soulless as the philosophy that brought it about.

On another note, I'm incredibly curious about what Chesterton would have thought of Kraft singles, and if they would have driven him mad.

MY FORTHCOMING WORK in five volumes, "The Neglect of Cheese in European Literature" is a work of such unprecedented and laborious detail that it is doubtful if I shall live to finish it. Some overflowings from such a fountain of information may therefore be permitted to sprinkle these pages. I cannot yet wholly explain the neglect to which I refer. Poets have been mysteriously silent on the subject of cheese.

Virgil[1], if I remember right, refers to it several times, but with too much Roman restraint. He does not let himself go on cheese. The only other poet I can think of just now who seems to have had some sensibility on the point was the nameless author of the nursery rhyme which says: "If all the trees were bread and cheese"—which is, indeed a rich and gigantic vision of the higher gluttony. If all the trees were bread and cheese there would be considerable deforestation in any part of England where I was living. Wild and wide woodlands would reel and fade before me as rapidly as they ran after Orpheus[2]. Except Virgil and this anonymous rhymer, I can recall no verse about cheese.

Yet it has every quality which we require in exalted poetry. It is a short, strong word; it rhymes to "breeze" and "seas" (an essential point); that it is emphatic in sound is admitted even by the civilization of the modern cities. For their citizens, with no apparent intention except emphasis, will often say, "Cheese it!" or even "Quite the cheese." The substance itself is imaginative. It

---

1. An ancient Roman poet of the Augustan period. He wrote three of the most famous poems in Latin literature: the Eclogues, the Georgics, and the epic Aeneid.

2. A legendary poet, musician, and prophet in ancient Greek literature. He was said to have had the ability to charm all living things and even stones with his music.

is ancient—sometimes in the individual case, always in the type and custom. It is simple, being directly derived from milk, which is one of the ancestral drinks, not lightly to be corrupted with soda-water. You know, I hope (though I myself have only just thought of it), that the four rivers of Eden were milk, water, wine, and ale. Aerated waters only appeared after the Fall.

But cheese has another quality, which is also the very soul of song. Once in endeavouring to lecture in several places at once, I made an eccentric journey across England, a journey of so irregular and even illogical shape that it necessitated my having lunch on four successive days in four roadside inns in four different counties. In each inn they had nothing but bread and cheese; nor can I imagine why a man should want more than bread and cheese, if he can get enough of it. In each inn the cheese was good; and in each inn it was different. There was a noble Wensleydale cheese in Yorkshire, a Cheshire cheese in Cheshire, and so on. Now, it is just here that true poetic civilization differs from that paltry and mechanical civilization which holds us all in bondage. Bad customs are universal and rigid, like modern militarism. Good customs are universal and varied, like native chivalry and self-defence. Both the good and bad civilization cover us as with a canopy, and protect us from all that is outside. But a good civilization spreads over us freely like a tree, varying and yielding because it is alive. A bad civilization stands up and sticks out above us like an umbrella—artificial, mathematical in shape; not merely universal, but uniform. So it is with the contrast between the substances that vary and the substances that are the same wherever they penetrate. By a wise doom of heaven men were commanded to eat cheese, but not the same cheese. Being really universal it varies from valley to valley. But if, let us say, we compare cheese with soap (that vastly inferior substance), we shall see that soap tends more and more to be merely Smith's Soap or Brown's Soap, sent automatically all over the world. If the Red Indians have soap it is Smith's Soap. If the Grand Lama has soap it is Brown's soap. There is nothing subtly and strangely Buddhist, nothing tenderly Tibetan, about his soap. I fancy the Grand Lama does not eat cheese (he is not worthy), but if he does it is probably a local cheese, having some real relation to his life and outlook. Safety matches, tinned foods, patent medicines are sent all over the world; but they are not produced all over the world. Therefore there is in them a mere dead identity, never that soft play of slight variation which exists in things produced everywhere out of the soil, in the milk of the kine, or the fruits of the orchard. You can get a whisky and soda at every outpost of the Empire: that is why so many Empire-builders go mad. But you are not tasting or touching any environment, as in the cider of Devonshire or the grapes of the Rhine. You are not approaching Nature in one of her myriad tints of mood, as in the holy act of eating cheese.

When I had done my pilgrimage in the four wayside public-houses I reached one of the great northern cities, and there I proceeded, with great rapidity and complete inconsistency, to a large and elaborate restaurant, where I knew I could get many other things besides bread and cheese. I could get that also, however; or at least I expected to get it; but I was sharply reminded that I had entered Babylon, and left England behind. The waiter brought me cheese, indeed, but cheese cut up into contemptibly small pieces; and it is the awful fact that, instead of Christian bread, he brought me biscuits[3]. Biscuits—to one who had eaten the cheese of four great countrysides! Biscuits—to one who had proved anew for himself the sanctity of the ancient wedding between cheese and bread! I addressed the waiter in warm and moving terms. I asked him who he was that he should put asunder those whom Humanity had joined. I asked him if he did not feel, as an artist, that a solid but yielding substance like cheese went naturally with a solid, yielding substance like bread; to eat it off biscuits is like eating it off slates. I asked him if, when he said his prayers, he was so supercilious as to pray for his daily biscuits. He gave me generally to understand that he was only obeying a custom of Modern Society. I have therefore resolved to raise my voice, not against the waiter, but against Modern Society, for this huge and unparalleled modern wrong.

---

3. He means crackers. They're called crackers, sir.

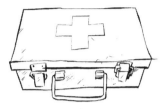

The Medical Mistake

What's Wrong With The World (**1910**)

"What is wrong is that we do not ask what is right."

THIS IS THE first chapter of Chesterton's *What Is Wrong With The World*. Chesterton expressed in other writings that the title of the book was not his idea but the publisher's. He once answered the question, "What is wrong with the world?" with a famous and familiar answer: "Dear Sirs, I am. Yours, G.K. Chesterton."

He deals in this chapter with how impossible it is to even attempt to talk about what is wrong with the world because none of us can agree on what a healthy, good world looks like. There is no use speaking of social remedies when we have conflicting visions of what illness is being cured... and what "cured" even means.

It's a simple concept but an important one to keep in mind when you find yourself trying to debate someone's views of how to fix things. They may not want the same outcome you do.

A BOOK OF modern social inquiry has a shape that is somewhat sharply defined. It begins as a rule with an analysis, with statistics, tables of population, decrease of crime among Congregationalists, growth of hysteria among policemen, and similar ascertained facts; it ends with a chapter that is generally called "The Remedy." It is almost wholly due to this careful, solid, and scientific method that "The Remedy" is never found. For this scheme of medical question and answer is a blunder; the first great blunder of sociology. It is always called stating the disease before we find the cure. But it is the whole definition and dignity of man that in social matters we must actually find the cure before we find the disease.

The fallacy is one of the fifty fallacies that come from the modern madness for biological or bodily metaphors. It is convenient to speak of the Social Organism, just as it is convenient to speak of the British Lion. But Britain is no more an organism than Britain is a lion. The moment we begin to give a nation the unity and simplicity of an animal, we begin to think wildly. Because every man is a biped, fifty men are not a centipede. This has produced, for instance, the gaping absurdity of perpetually talking about "young nations" and "dying nations," as if a nation had a fixed and physical span of life. Thus people will say that Spain has entered a final senility; they might as well say that Spain is losing all her teeth. Or people will say that Canada should soon produce a literature; which is like saying that Canada must soon grow a new moustache. Nations consist of people; the first generation may be decrepit, or the ten thousandth may be vigorous. Similar applications of the fallacy are made by those who see in the increasing size of national possessions, a simple increase in wisdom and stature, and in favor with God and man. These people, indeed, even fall short in subtlety of the parallel of a human body. They do not even ask whether an empire is growing taller in its youth, or only growing fatter in its old age. But of all the instances of error arising from this physical fancy, the worst is that we have before us: the habit of exhaustively describing a social sickness, and then propounding a social drug.

Now we do talk first about the disease in cases of bodily breakdown; and that for an excellent reason. Because, though there may be doubt about the way in which the body broke down, there is no doubt at all about the shape in which it should be built up again. No doctor proposes to produce a new kind of man, with a new arrangement of eyes or limbs. The hospital, by necessity, may send a man home with one leg less: but it will not (in a creative rapture) send him home with one leg extra. Medical science is content with the normal human body, and only seeks to restore it.

But social science is by no means always content with the normal human soul; it has all sorts of fancy souls for sale. Man as a social idealist will say "I am tired of being a Puritan; I want to be a Pagan," or "Beyond this dark probation of Individualism I see the shining paradise of Collectivism." Now in bodily ills there is none of this difference about the ultimate ideal. The patient may or may not want quinine[1]; but he certainly wants health. No one says "I am tired of this headache; I want some toothache," or "The only thing for this Russian influenza is a few German measles," or "Through this dark probation of catarrh[2] I see the shining paradise of rheumatism." But exactly the whole difficulty in our public problems is that some men are aiming at cures which other men would regard as worse maladies; are offering ultimate conditions as states of health which others would uncompromisingly call states of disease. Mr. Belloc[3] once said that he would no more part with the idea of property than with his teeth; yet to Mr. Bernard Shaw[4] property is not

---

1. Anti-parasite medication used to treat malaria.

2. Excessive discharge or buildup of mucus in the nose or throat, associated with inflammation of the mucous membrane. Ew.

3. Hillaire Belloc was a contemporary and friend of Chesterton. He was another popular Catholic writer and historian. Many Chesterton fans are also Belloc fans though I admit I have not read much of his stuff. Chesterton brings him up often.

4. George Bernard Shaw was another contemporary of Chesterton. He was a playwright and an avowed atheist. He and Chesterton had a great friendship despite disagreeing on nearly everything. Shaw is also mentioned quite often in Chesterton's work.

a tooth, but a toothache. Lord Milner[5] has sincerely attempted to introduce German efficiency; and many of us would as soon welcome German measles. Dr. Saleeby[6] would honestly like to have Eugenics; but I would rather have rheumatics.

This is the arresting and dominant fact about modern social discussion; that the quarrel is not merely about the difficulties, but about the aim. We agree about the evil; it is about the good that we should tear each other's eyes out. We all admit that a lazy aristocracy is a bad thing. We should not by any means all admit that an active aristocracy would be a good thing. We all feel angry with an irreligious priesthood; but some of us would go mad with disgust at a really religious one. Everyone is indignant if our army is weak, including the people who would be even more indignant if it were strong. The social case is exactly the opposite of the medical case. We do not disagree, like doctors, about the precise nature of the illness, while agreeing about the nature of health. On the contrary, we all agree that England is unhealthy, but half of us would not look at her in what the other half would call blooming health. Public abuses are so prominent and pestilent that they sweep all generous people into a sort of fictitious unanimity. We forget that, while we agree about the abuses of things, we should differ very much about the uses of them. Mr. Cadbury[7] and I would agree about the bad public house. It would be precisely in front of the good public-house that our painful personal fracas would occur.

I maintain, therefore, that the common sociological method is quite useless: that of first dissecting abject poverty or cataloguing prostitution. We all dislike abject poverty; but it might be another business if we began to discuss independent and dignified poverty. We all disapprove of prostitution; but we

---

5. 1st Viscount Milner, KG, GCB, GCMG, PC (whatever that means) was a British statesman and colonial administrator who played a role in the formulation of foreign and domestic policy between the mid-1890s and early 1920s.

6. Caleb Williams Saleeby was an English physician, writer, and journalist known for his support of eugenics. During World War I, he was an adviser to the Minister of Food and advocated the establishment of a Ministry of Health.

7. Pretty sure this is John Cadbury of Cadbury Eggs fame. He was a Quaker (therefore a teetotaler and pacifist) and a rich philanthropist.

do not all approve of purity. The only way to discuss the social evil is to get at once to the social ideal. We can all see the national madness; but what is national sanity? I have called this book "What Is Wrong with the World?" and the upshot of the title can be easily and clearly stated. What is wrong is that we do not ask what is right.

The Maniac

Orthodoxy (**1908**)

"The madman is not the man who has lost his reason. The madman is the man who has lost everything except his reason."

YET ANOTHER FIRST chapter, this time from one of Chesterton's most famous books, *Orthodoxy*. For many, *Orthodoxy* is the first Chesterton book they attempt to read, and many do not finish. This is because it is hard to follow Chesterton through a whole book unless you have grown accustomed to the way he thinks and writes.

While Orthodoxy is definitely one of Chesterton's greatest books, it is a tough read for someone seeking out a methodical and straightforward work of apologetics. Chesterton didn't write point-by-point systems of thought. He presented various ideas that led him in a certain direction. He painted a picture but left it up to the reader to find the conclusions. One reason for that is found in this chapter. He says it is the mad man who creates a perfect air-tight system of thought that fits everything in the universe into it, casting out all skepticism and creating a false sense of confidence. A critical piece of Chesterton's philosophy is mystery, for without mystery there is no romance.

In this chapter, Chesterton introduces the idea of the madman's circle which he compares to the symbol of the cross. One closes in on itself, is tidy, circular, and contained. The cross is forever open with a paradox at the center. His fictional work, one of my favorites of his *The Ball And The Cross*, attempts to pit these philosophies against each other in a buddy comedy about a Catholic and an atheist. It's an illustration he uses often, so it is good to know what he means whenever he uses the term "circular." It's also incredibly helpful in discerning incomplete and empty philosophies that seem to solve all riddles while simultaneously ignoring the deeper mysteries of life.

THOROUGHLY WORLDLY PEOPLE never understand even the world; they rely altogether on a few cynical maxims which are not true. Once I remember walking with a prosperous publisher, who made a remark which I had often heard before; it is, indeed, almost a motto of the modern world. Yet I had heard it once too often, and I saw suddenly that there was nothing in it. The publisher said of somebody, "That man will get on; he believes in himself." And I remember that as I lifted my head to listen, my eye caught an omnibus on which was written "Hanwell[1]." I said to him, "Shall I tell you where the men are who believe most in themselves? For I can tell you. I know of men who believe in themselves more colossally than Napoleon or Caesar. I know where flames the fixed star of certainty and success. I can guide you to the thrones of the Super-men. The men who really believe in themselves are all in lunatic asylums."

He said mildly that there were a good many men after all who believed in themselves and who were not in lunatic asylums. "Yes, there are," I retorted, "and you of all men ought to know them. That drunken poet from whom you would not take a dreary tragedy, he believed in himself. That elderly minister with an epic from whom you were hiding in a back room, he believed in

---

1. St Bernard's Hospital, also known as Hanwell Insane Asylum and the Hanwell Pauper and Lunatic Asylum, was built for the pauper insane, opening as the First Middlesex County Asylum in 1831.

himself. If you consulted your business experience instead of your ugly indi-vidualistic philosophy, you would know that believing in himself is one of the commonest signs of a rotter. Actors who can't act believe in themselves; and debtors who won't pay. It would be much truer to say that a man will certainly fail, because he believes in himself. Complete self-confidence is not merely a sin; complete self-confidence is a weakness. Believing utterly in one's self is a hysterical and superstitious belief like believing in Joanna Southcote[2]: the man who has it has 'Hanwell' written on his face as plain as it is written on that omnibus." And to all this my friend the publisher made this very deep and effective reply, "Well, if a man is not to believe in himself, in what is he to believe?" After a long pause I replied, "I will go home and write a book in answer to that question." This is the book that I have written in answer to it.

But I think this book may well start where our argument started— in the neighbourhood of the mad-house. Modern masters of science are much impressed with the need of beginning all inquiry with a fact. The ancient masters of religion were quite equally impressed with that necessity. They began with the fact of sin—a fact as practical as potatoes. Whether or no man could be washed in miraculous waters, there was no doubt at any rate that he wanted washing. But certain religious leaders in London, not mere materialists, have begun in our day not to deny the highly disputable water,

---

2. Joanna Southcott (I believe Chesterton had the spelling wrong here) believed that she possessed supernatural gifts, she wrote prophecies in rhyme and announced herself as the Woman of the Apocalypse spoken of in Revelation (12:1-6). She sold paper "seals of the Lord" which secured a place among the 144,000 people who would be elected to eternal life.
(OK sorry I know this is a long footnote but wow this is crazy)
　　At the age of 64 Southcott affirmed that she was pregnant and would be giving birth to the new Mes-siah. On the day the messiah was to be born Southcott was in a trance. Turns out she had a disorder which gave her the appearance of being pregnant and this fuelled her followers, who reached a number of around 100,000 in 1814, mainly in the London area.
　　The official date of her death was given as 27 December 1814, but she likely died the previous day, as her followers retained her body for some time in the belief that she would be raised from the dead. They agreed to her burial only after the corpse began to decay
　　Her followers continued to believe in her after her death and were said to have numbered over 100,000. In 1881 there was an enclave of Southcott followers living in the Chatham area who were distin-guished by their long beards and good manners.
　　Southcott left a sealed wooden box of prophecies with the instruction that it be opened only at a time of national crisis, and then only in the presence of all the 24 bishops of the Church of England. As far as we know it has never been opened. Many fakes have been created and nobody seems to know where the real one went.
　　Southcott prophesied that the Day of Judgement would come in the year 2004.

Wow. What a deep dive.

but to deny the indisputable dirt. Certain new theologians dispute original sin, which is the only part of Christian theology which can really be proved. Some followers of the Reverend R.J.Campbell[3], in their almost too fastidious spirituality, admit divine sinlessness, which they cannot see even in their dreams. But they essentially deny human sin, which they can see in the street. The strongest saints and the strongest skeptics alike took positive evil as the starting-point of their argument. If it be true (as it certainly is) that a man can feel exquisite happiness in skinning a cat, then the religious philosopher can only draw one of two deductions. He must either deny the existence of God, as all atheists do; or he must deny the present union between God and man, as all Christians do. The new theologians seem to think it a highly rationalistic solution to deny the cat.

In this remarkable situation it is plainly not now possible (with any hope of a universal appeal) to start, as our fathers did, with the fact of sin. This very fact which was to them (and is to me) as plain as a pikestaff, is the very fact that has been specially diluted or denied. But though moderns deny the existence of sin, I do not think that they have yet denied the existence of a lunatic asylum. We all agree still that there is a collapse of the intellect as unmistakable as a falling house. Men deny hell, but not, as yet, Hanwell. For the purpose of our primary argument the one may very well stand where the other stood. I mean that as all thoughts and theories were once judged by whether they tended to make a man lose his soul, so for our present purpose all modern thoughts and theories may be judged by whether they tend to make a man lose his wits.

It is true that some speak lightly and loosely of insanity as in itself attractive. But a moment's thought will show that if disease is beautiful, it is generally some one else's disease. A blind man may be picturesque; but it requires two eyes to see the picture. And similarly even the wildest poetry of

3. Reginald John Campbell was a British Congregationalist and Anglican divine who became a popular preacher while the minister at the City Temple and a leading exponent of 'The New Theology' movement of 1907. He was a socialist and it seems he was not a believer in the infallibility of scripture. He ended up believing in reincarnation later, after this book was written. Sort of like an 1800's Rob Bell or something.

insanity can only be enjoyed by the sane. To the insane man his insanity is quite prosaic, because it is quite true. A man who thinks himself a chicken is to himself as ordinary as a chicken. A man who thinks he is a bit of glass is to himself as dull as a bit of glass. It is the homogeneity of his mind which makes him dull, and which makes him mad. It is only because we see the irony of his idea that we think him even amusing; it is only because he does not see the irony of his idea that he is put in Hanwell at all.

In short, oddities only strike ordinary people. Oddities do not strike odd people. This is why ordinary people have a much more exciting time; while odd people are always complaining of the dullness of life. This is also why the new novels die so quickly, and why the old fairy tales endure for ever. The old fairy tale makes the hero a normal human boy; it is his adventures that are startling; they startle him because he is normal. But in the modern psychological novel the hero is abnormal; the centre is not central. Hence the fiercest adventures fail to affect him adequately, and the book is monotonous. You can make a story out of a hero among dragons; but not out of a dragon among dragons. The fairy tale discusses what a sane man will do in a mad world. The sober realistic novel of to-day discusses what an essential lunatic will do in a dull world.

Let us begin, then, with the mad-house; from this evil and fantastic inn let us set forth on our intellectual journey. Now, if we are to glance at the philosophy of sanity, the first thing to do in the matter is to blot out one big and common mistake. There is a notion adrift everywhere that imagination, especially mystical imagination, is dangerous to man's mental balance. Poets are commonly spoken of as psychologically unreliable; and generally there is a vague association between wreathing laurels in your hair and sticking straws in it. Facts and history utterly contradict this view. Most of the very great poets have been not only sane, but extremely business-like; and if Shakespeare ever really held horses, it was because he was much the safest man to hold them.

Imagination does not breed insanity. Exactly what does breed insanity is reason. Poets do not go mad; but chess-players do. Mathematicians go mad, and cashiers; but creative artists very seldom. I am not, as will be seen, in any sense attacking logic: I only say that this danger does lie in logic, not in imagination. Artistic paternity is as wholesome as physical paternity. Moreover, it is worthy of remark that when a poet really was morbid it was commonly because he had some weak spot of rationality on his brain. Poe[4], for instance, really was morbid; not because he was poetical, but because he was specially analytical. Even chess was too poetical for him; he disliked chess because it was full of knights and castles, like a poem. He avowedly preferred the black discs of draughts[5], because they were more like the mere black dots on a diagram.

Perhaps the strongest case of all is this: that only one great English poet went mad, Cowper[6]. And he was definitely driven mad by logic, by the ugly and alien logic of predestination. Poetry was not the disease, but the medicine; poetry partly kept him in health. He could sometimes forget the red and thirsty hell to which his hideous necessitarianism dragged him among the wide waters and the white flat lilies of the Ouse. He was damned by John Calvin[7]; he was almost saved by John Gilpin[8].

Everywhere we see that men do not go mad by dreaming. Critics are much madder than poets. Homer[9] is complete and calm enough; it is his critics who tear him into extravagant tatters. Shakespeare is quite himself; it is only some of his critics who have discovered that he was somebody else. And though St. John the Evangelist saw many strange monsters in his vision, he saw no creature so wild as one of his own commentators. The general fact is simple. Poetry is sane because it floats easily in an infinite sea; reason seeks

---

4. We all know Edgar Allen Poe right? I don't need a footnote for that guy. He's huge. He wrote scary stories.

5. Checkers. He means checkers.

6. William Cowper was an English poet and hymn writer. Cowper changed the direction of 18th-century nature poetry by writing of everyday life and scenes of the English countryside. In many ways, he was one of the forerunners of Romantic poetry. After being institutionalized for insanity, Cowper found refuge in a fervent evangelical Christianity. He continued to suffer doubt and, after a dream in 1773, believed that he was doomed to eternal damnation. He recovered and wrote more religious hymns.

7. Come on, we all know John Calvin. Hipster beard, IPA, smokes a pipe, TULIP, etc.

8. John Gilpin was a character in Cowper's comic ballad "The Diverting History of John Gilpin Shewing how he went Farther than he intended, and came safe Home again" written in 1782.].

9. Writer of the Iliad, not patriarch of the Simpsons.

to cross the infinite sea, and so make it finite. The result is mental exhaustion, like the physical exhaustion of Mr. Holbein[10]. To accept everything is an exercise, to understand everything a strain. The poet only desires exaltation and expansion, a world to stretch himself in. The poet only asks to get his head into the heavens. It is the logician who seeks to get the heavens into his head. And it is his head that splits.

It is a small matter, but not irrelevant, that this striking mistake is commonly supported by a striking misquotation. We have all heard people cite the celebrated line of Dryden[11] as "Great genius is to madness near allied." But Dryden did not say that great genius was to madness near allied. Dryden was a great genius himself, and knew better. It would have been hard to find a man more romantic than he, or more sensible. What Dryden said was this, "Great wits are oft to madness near allied"; and that is true. It is the pure promptitude of the intellect that is in peril of a breakdown. Also people might remember of what sort of man Dryden was talking. He was not talking of any unworldly visionary like Vaughan[12] or George Herbert[13]. He was talking of a cynical man of the world, a sceptic, a diplomatist, a great practical politician. Such men are indeed to madness near allied. Their incessant calculation of their own brains and other people's brains is a dangerous trade. It is always perilous to the mind to reckon up the mind. A flippant person has asked why we say, "As mad as a hatter." A more flippant person might answer that a hatter is mad because he has to measure the human head.

And if great reasoners are often maniacal, it is equally true that maniacs are commonly great reasoners. When I was engaged in a controversy with the CLARION[14] on the matter of free will, that able writer Mr. R.B.Suthers

10. Hans Holbein is the only person I can find who this might be, a famous artist who was highly accomplished and prolific, but I don't know what the physical exhaustion here is referring to.

11. John Dryden was an English poet, literary critic, translator, and playwright who was appointed England's first Poet Laureate in 1668.

12. Possibly referring to Henry Vaughan. A Welsh metaphysical poet, author, physician, and translator. He is best known for religious poetry published in *Silex Scintillans* in 1650, with a second part in 1655.

13. Welsh-born poet, orator, and priest of the Church of England.

14. The Clarion was a weekly newspaper published by Robert Blatchford, based in the United Kingdom. It was a socialist publication with a Britain-focused rather than internationalist perspective on political affairs, as seen in its support of the British involvement in the Anglo-Boer Wars and the First World War.

said that free will was lunacy, because it meant causeless actions, and the actions of a lunatic would be causeless. I do not dwell here upon the disastrous lapse in determinist logic. Obviously if any actions, even a lunatic's, can be causeless, determinism is done for. If the chain of causation can be broken for a madman, it can be broken for a man. But my purpose is to point out something more practical.

It was natural, perhaps, that a modern Marxian Socialist should not know anything about free will. But it was certainly remarkable that a modern Marxian Socialist should not know anything about lunatics. Mr. Suthers evidently did not know anything about lunatics. The last thing that can be said of a lunatic is that his actions are causeless. If any human acts may loosely be called causeless, they are the minor acts of a healthy man; whistling as he walks; slashing the grass with a stick; kicking his heels or rubbing his hands. It is the happy man who does the useless things; the sick man is not strong enough to be idle. It is exactly such careless and causeless actions that the madman could never understand; for the madman (like the determinist) generally sees too much cause in everything. The madman would read a conspiratorial significance into those empty activities. He would think that the lopping of the grass was an attack on private property. He would think that the kicking of the heels was a signal to an accomplice. If the madman could for an instant become careless, he would become sane.

Every one who has had the misfortune to talk with people in the heart or on the edge of mental disorder, knows that their most sinister quality is a horrible clarity of detail; a connecting of one thing with another in a map more elaborate than a maze. If you argue with a madman, it is extremely probable that you will get the worst of it; for in many ways his mind moves all the quicker for not being delayed by the things that go with good judgment. He is not hampered by a sense of humour or by charity, or by the dumb certainties of experience. He is the more logical for losing certain sane affections. Indeed, the common phrase for insanity is in this respect a misleading one. The madman is not the man who has lost his reason. The madman is the man who has lost everything except his reason.

The madman's explanation of a thing is always complete, and often in a purely rational sense satisfactory. Or, to speak more strictly, the insane explanation, if not conclusive, is at least unanswerable; this may be observed specially in the two or three commonest kinds of madness. If a man says (for instance) that men have a conspiracy against him, you cannot dispute it except by saying that all the men deny that they are conspirators; which is exactly what conspirators would do. His explanation covers the facts as much as yours. Or if a man says that he is the rightful King of England, it is no complete answer to say that the existing authorities call him mad; for if he were King of England that might be the wisest thing for the existing authorities to do. Or if a man says that he is Jesus Christ, it is no answer to tell him that the world denies his divinity; for the world denied Christ's.

Nevertheless he is wrong. But if we attempt to trace his error in exact terms, we shall not find it quite so easy as we had supposed. Perhaps the nearest we can get to expressing it is to say this: that his mind moves in a perfect but narrow circle. A small circle is quite as infinite as a large circle; but, though it is quite as infinite, it is not so large. In the same way the insane explanation is quite as complete as the sane one, but it is not so large. A bullet is quite as round as the world, but it is not the world. There is such a thing as a narrow universality; there is such a thing as a small and cramped eternity; you may see it in many modern religions.

Now, speaking quite externally and empirically, we may say that the strongest and most unmistakable MARK of madness is this combination between a logical completeness and a spiritual contraction. The lunatic's theory explains a large number of things, but it does not explain them in a large way. I mean that if you or I were dealing with a mind that was growing morbid, we should be chiefly concerned not so much to give it arguments as to give it air, to convince it that there was something cleaner and cooler outside the suffocation of a single argument.

Suppose, for instance, it were the first case that I took as typical; suppose it were the case of a man who accused everybody of conspiring against him. If we could express our deepest feelings of protest and appeal against this obsession, I suppose we should say something like this: "Oh, I admit that you have your case and have it by heart, and that many things do fit into other things as you say. I admit that your explanation explains a great deal; but what a great deal it leaves out! Are there no other stories in the world except yours; and are all men busy with your business? Suppose we grant the details; perhaps when the man in the street did not seem to see you it was only his cunning; perhaps when the policeman asked you your name it was only because he knew it already. But how much happier you would be if you only knew that these people cared nothing about you! How much larger your life would be if your self could become smaller in it; if you could really look at other men with common curiosity and pleasure; if you could see them walking as they are in their sunny selfishness and their virile indifference! You would begin to be interested in them, because they were not interested in you. You would break out of this tiny and tawdry theatre in which your own little plot is always being played, and you would find yourself under a freer sky, in a street full of splendid strangers."

Or suppose it were the second case of madness, that of a man who claims the crown, your impulse would be to answer, "All right! Perhaps you know that you are the King of England; but why do you care? Make one magnificent effort and you will be a human being and look down on all the kings of the earth."

Or it might be the third case, of the madman who called himself Christ. If we said what we felt, we should say, "So you are the Creator and Redeemer of the world: but what a small world it must be! What a little heaven you must inhabit, with angels no bigger than butterflies! How sad it must be to be God; and an inadequate God! Is there really no life fuller and no love more marvellous than yours; and is it really in your small and painful pity that all flesh must put its faith? How much happier you would be, how much more of you there would be, if the hammer of a higher God could smash your small cosmos, scattering the stars like spangles, and leave you in the open, free like other men to look up as well as down!"

And it must be remembered that the most purely practical science does take this view of mental evil; it does not seek to argue with it like a heresy but simply to snap it like a spell. Neither modern science nor ancient religion believes in complete free thought. Theology rebukes certain thoughts by calling them blasphemous. Science rebukes certain thoughts by calling them morbid. For example, some religious societies discouraged men more or less from thinking about sex. The new scientific society definitely discourages men from thinking about death; it is a fact, but it is considered a morbid fact. And in dealing with those whose morbidity has a touch of mania, modern science cares far less for pure logic than a dancing Dervish.

In these cases it is not enough that the unhappy man should desire truth; he must desire health. Nothing can save him but a blind hunger for normality, like that of a beast. A man cannot think himself out of mental evil; for it is actually the organ of thought that has become diseased, ungovernable, and, as it were, independent. He can only be saved by will or faith. The moment his mere reason moves, it moves in the old circular rut; he will go round and round his logical circle, just as a man in a third-class carriage on the Inner Circle will go round and round the Inner Circle unless he performs the voluntary, vigorous, and mystical act of getting out at Gower Street. Decision is the whole business here; a door must be shut for ever. Every remedy is a desperate remedy. Every cure is a miraculous cure. Curing a madman is not arguing with a philosopher; it is casting out a devil. And however quietly doctors and psychologists may go to work in the matter, their attitude is profoundly intolerant— as intolerant as Bloody Mary. Their attitude is really this: that the man must stop thinking, if he is to go on living. Their counsel is one of intellectual amputation. If thy HEAD offend thee, cut it off; for it is better, not merely to enter the Kingdom of Heaven as a child, but to enter it as an imbecile, rather than with your whole intellect to be cast into hell— or into Hanwell.

Such is the madman of experience; he is commonly a reasoner, frequently a successful reasoner. Doubtless he could be vanquished in mere reason, and the case against him put logically. But it can be put much more precisely in more general and even aesthetic terms. He is in the clean and well-lit prison of one idea: he is sharpened to one painful point. He is without healthy hesitation and healthy complexity.

Now, as I explain in the introduction, I have determined in these early chapters to give not so much a diagram of a doctrine as some pictures of a point of view. And I have described at length my vision of the maniac for this reason: that just as I am affected by the maniac, so I am affected by most modern thinkers. That unmistakable mood or note that I hear from Hanwell, I hear also from half the chairs of science and seats of learning to-day; and most of the mad doctors are mad doctors in more senses than one. They all have exactly that combination we have noted: the combination of an expansive and exhaustive reason with a contracted common sense. They are universal only in the sense that they take one thin explanation and carry it very far. But a pattern can stretch for ever and still be a small pattern. They see a chess-board white on black, and if the universe is paved with it, it is still white on black. Like the lunatic, they cannot alter their standpoint; they cannot make a mental effort and suddenly see it black on white.

Take first the more obvious case of materialism. As an explanation of the world, materialism has a sort of insane simplicity. It has just the quality of the madman's argument; we have at once the sense of it covering everything and the sense of it leaving everything out. Contemplate some able and sincere materialist, as, for instance, Mr. McCabe[15], and you will have exactly this unique sensation. He understands everything, and everything does not seem worth understanding. His cosmos may be complete in every rivet and cog-wheel, but still his cosmos is smaller than our world. Somehow his scheme, like the lucid scheme of the madman, seems unconscious of the alien energies and the large indifference of the earth; it is not thinking of the real things of the earth, of fighting peoples or proud mothers, or first love or fear upon the sea. The earth is so very large, and the cosmos is so very small. The cosmos is about the smallest hole that a man can hide his head in.

It must be understood that I am not now discussing the relation of these creeds to truth; but, for the present, solely their relation to health. Later in the argument I hope to attack the question of objective verity; here I speak only of a phenomenon of psychology. I do not for the present attempt to

---

15. Joseph Martin McCabe was an English writer and speaker on freethought, after having been a Roman Catholic priest earlier in his life. McCabe joined groups such as the Rationalist Association and the National Secular Society. He criticised Christianity from a rationalist perspective, but also was involved in the South Place Ethical Society which grew out of dissenting Protestantism and was a precursor of modern secular humanism.

prove to Haeckel[16] that materialism is untrue, any more than I attempted to prove to the man who thought he was Christ that he was labouring under an error. I merely remark here on the fact that both cases have the same kind of completeness and the same kind of incompleteness. You can explain a man's detention at Hanwell by an indifferent public by saying that it is the crucifixion of a god of whom the world is not worthy. The explanation does explain. Similarly you may explain the order in the universe by saying that all things, even the souls of men, are leaves inevitably unfolding on an utterly unconscious tree— the blind destiny of matter. The explanation does explain, though not, of course, so completely as the madman's. But the point here is that the normal human mind not only objects to both, but feels to both the same objection. Its approximate statement is that if the man in Hanwell is the real God, he is not much of a god. And, similarly, if the cosmos of the materialist is the real cosmos, it is not much of a cosmos. The thing has shrunk. The deity is less divine than many men; and (according to Haeckel) the whole of life is something much more grey, narrow, and trivial than many separate aspects of it. The parts seem greater than the whole.

For we must remember that the materialist philosophy (whether true or not) is certainly much more limiting than any religion. In one sense, of course, all intelligent ideas are narrow. They cannot be broader than themselves. A Christian is only restricted in the same sense that an atheist is restricted. He cannot think Christianity false and continue to be a Christian; and the atheist cannot think atheism false and continue to be an atheist. But as it happens, there is a very special sense in which materialism has more restrictions than spiritualism. Mr. McCabe thinks me a slave because I am not allowed to believe in determinism. I think Mr. McCabe a slave because he is not allowed to believe in fairies. But if we examine the two vetoes we shall see that his is really much more of a pure veto than mine.

---

16. Ernst Heinrich Philipp August Haeckel was a German zoologist, naturalist, eugenicist, philosopher, physician, professor, marine biologist, and artist who discovered, described and named thousands of new species, mapped a genealogical tree relating all life forms, and coined many terms in biology, including ecology, phylum, phylogeny, and Protista. Haeckel promoted and popularised Charles Darwin's work in Germany.

Haeckel was also a promoter of scientific racism and embraced the idea of Social Darwinism.

The Christian is quite free to believe that there is a considerable amount of settled order and inevitable development in the universe. But the materialist is not allowed to admit into his spotless machine the slightest speck of spiritualism or miracle. Poor Mr. McCabe is not allowed to retain even the tiniest imp, though it might be hiding in a pimpernel. The Christian admits that the universe is manifold and even miscellaneous, just as a sane man knows that he is complex. The sane man knows that he has a touch of the beast, a touch of the devil, a touch of the saint, a touch of the citizen. Nay, the really sane man knows that he has a touch of the madman. But the materialist's world is quite simple and solid, just as the madman is quite sure he is sane. The materialist is sure that history has been simply and solely a chain of causation, just as the interesting person before mentioned is quite sure that he is simply and solely a chicken. Materialists and madmen never have doubts.

Spiritual doctrines do not actually limit the mind as do materialistic denials. Even if I believe in immortality I need not think about it. But if I disbelieve in immortality I must not think about it. In the first case the road is open and I can go as far as I like; in the second the road is shut. But the case is even stronger, and the parallel with madness is yet more strange. For it was our case against the exhaustive and logical theory of the lunatic that, right or wrong, it gradually destroyed his humanity. Now it is the charge against the main deductions of the materialist that, right or wrong, they gradually destroy his humanity; I do not mean only kindness, I mean hope, courage, poetry, initiative, all that is human.

For instance, when materialism leads men to complete fatalism (as it generally does), it is quite idle to pretend that it is in any sense a liberating force. It is absurd to say that you are especially advancing freedom when you only use free thought to destroy free will. The determinists come to bind, not to loose. They may well call their law the "chain" of causation. It is the worst chain that ever fettered a human being. You may use the language of liberty, if you like, about materialistic teaching, but it is obvious that this is just as inapplicable to it as a whole as the same language when applied to a man locked up in a mad-house. You may say, if you like, that the man is free to think himself a poached egg. But it is surely a more massive and important fact that if he is a poached egg he is not free to eat, drink, sleep, walk, or smoke a cigarette. Similarly you may say, if you like, that the bold determinist speculator is free to disbelieve in the reality of the will. But it is a much more massive and important fact that he is not free to raise, to curse, to thank, to justify, to urge, to punish, to resist temptations, to incite mobs, to make New Year resolutions, to pardon sinners, to rebuke tyrants, or even to say "thank you" for the mustard.

In passing from this subject I may note that there is a queer fallacy to the effect that materialistic fatalism is in some way favourable to mercy, to the abolition of cruel punishments or punishments of any kind. This is startlingly the reverse of the truth. It is quite tenable that the doctrine of necessity makes no difference at all; that it leaves the flogger flogging and the kind friend exhorting as before. But obviously if it stops either of them it stops the kind exhortation. That the sins are inevitable does not prevent punishment; if it prevents anything it prevents persuasion.

Determinism is quite as likely to lead to cruelty as it is certain to lead to cowardice. Determinism is not inconsistent with the cruel treatment of criminals. What it is (perhaps) inconsistent with is the generous treatment of criminals; with any appeal to their better feelings or encouragement in their moral struggle. The determinist does not believe in appealing to the will, but he does believe in changing the environment. He must not say to the sinner, "Go and sin no more," because the sinner cannot help it. But he can put him in boiling oil; for boiling oil is an environment. Considered as a figure, therefore, the materialist has the fantastic outline of the figure of the madman. Both take up a position at once unanswerable and intolerable.

Of course it is not only of the materialist that all this is true. The same would apply to the other extreme of speculative logic. There is a sceptic far more terrible than he who believes that everything began in matter. It is possible to meet the sceptic who believes that everything began in himself. He doubts not the existence of angels or devils, but the existence of men and cows. For him his own friends are a mythology made up by himself. He created his own father and his own mother. This horrible fancy has in it something decidedly attractive to the somewhat mystical egoism of our day.

That publisher who thought that men would get on if they believed in themselves, those seekers after the Superman who are always looking for him in the looking-glass, those writers who talk about impressing their personalities instead of creating life for the world, all these people have really only an inch between them and this awful emptiness. Then when this kindly world all round the man has been blackened out like a lie; when friends fade into ghosts, and the foundations of the world fail; then when the man, believing in nothing and in no man, is alone in his own nightmare, then the great individualistic motto shall be written over him in avenging irony. The stars will be only dots in the blackness of his own brain; his mother's face will be only a sketch from his own insane pencil on the walls of his cell. But over his cell shall be written, with dreadful truth, "He believes in himself."

All that concerns us here, however, is to note that this panegoistic extreme of thought exhibits the same paradox as the other extreme of materialism. It is equally complete in theory and equally crippling in practice. For the sake of simplicity, it is easier to state the notion by saying that a man can believe that he is always in a dream. Now, obviously there can be no positive proof given to him that he is not in a dream, for the simple reason that no proof can be offered that might not be offered in a dream. But if the man began to burn down London and say that his housekeeper would soon call him to breakfast, we should take him and put him with other logicians in a place which has often been alluded to in the course of this chapter.

The man who cannot believe his senses, and the man who cannot believe anything else, are both insane, but their insanity is proved not by any error in their argument, but by the manifest mistake of their whole lives. They have both locked themselves up in two boxes, painted inside with the sun and stars; they are both unable to get out, the one into the health and happiness of heaven, the other even into the health and happiness of the earth.

Their position is quite reasonable; nay, in a sense it is infinitely reasonable, just as a threepenny bit is infinitely circular. But there is such a thing as a mean infinity, a base and slavish eternity. It is amusing to notice that many of the moderns, whether sceptics or mystics, have taken as their sign a certain eastern symbol, which is the very symbol of this ultimate nullity. When they wish to represent eternity, they represent it by a serpent with his tail in his mouth. There is a startling sarcasm in the image of that very unsatisfactory meal. The eternity of the material fatalists, the eternity of the eastern pessimists, the eternity of the supercilious theosophists[17] and higher scientists of to-day is, indeed, very well presented by a serpent eating his tail, a degraded animal who destroys even himself.

This chapter is purely practical and is concerned with what actually is the chief mark and element of insanity; we may say in summary that it is reason used without root, reason in the void. The man who begins to think without the proper first principles goes mad; he begins to think at the wrong end. And for the rest of these pages we have to try and discover what is the right end. But we may ask in conclusion, if this be what drives men mad, what is it that keeps them sane? By the end of this book I hope to give a definite, some will think a far too definite, answer.

But for the moment it is possible in the same solely practical manner to give a general answer touching what in actual human history keeps men sane. Mysticism keeps men sane. As long as you have mystery you have health; when you destroy mystery you create morbidity. The ordinary man has always been sane because the ordinary man has always been a mystic. He has permitted the twilight. He has always had one foot in earth and the other in fairyland.

---

17. Theosophy, occult movement originating in the 19th century with roots that can be traced to ancient Gnosticism and Neoplatonism. The term theosophy, derived from the Greek theos ("god") and sophia ("wisdom"), is generally understood to mean "divine wisdom." Forms of this doctrine were held in antiquity by the Manichaeans, an Iranian dualist sect, and in the Middle Ages by two groups of dualist heretics, the Bogomils in Bulgaria and the Byzantine Empire and the Cathari in southern France and Italy. In modern times, theosophical views have been held by Rosicrucians and by speculative Freemasons. The international New Age movement of the 1970s and '80s originated among independent theosophical groups in the United Kingdom.

Theosophy teaches that the purpose of human life is spiritual emancipation and claims that the human soul undergoes reincarnation upon bodily death according to a process of karma. It promotes values of universal brotherhood and social improvement, although it does not stipulate particular ethical codes.

He has always left himself free to doubt his gods; but (unlike the agnostic of to-day) free also to believe in them. He has always cared more for truth than for consistency. If he saw two truths that seemed to contradict each other, he would take the two truths and the contradiction along with them. His spiritual sight is stereoscopic, like his physical sight: he sees two different pictures at once and yet sees all the better for that. Thus he has always believed that there was such a thing as fate, but such a thing as free will also. Thus he believed that children were indeed the kingdom of heaven, but nevertheless ought to be obedient to the kingdom of earth. He admired youth because it was young and age because it was not.

It is exactly this balance of apparent contradictions that has been the whole buoyancy of the healthy man. The whole secret of mysticism is this: that man can understand everything by the help of what he does not understand. The morbid logician seeks to make everything lucid, and succeeds in making everything mysterious. The mystic allows one thing to be mysterious, and everything else becomes lucid. The determinist makes the theory of causation quite clear, and then finds that he cannot say "if you please" to the housemaid. The Christian permits free will to remain a sacred mystery; but because of this his relations with the housemaid become of a sparkling and crystal clearness. He puts the seed of dogma in a central darkness; but it branches forth in all directions with abounding natural health.

As we have taken the circle as the symbol of reason and madness, we may very well take the cross as the symbol at once of mystery and of health. Buddhism is centripetal, but Christianity is centrifugal[18]: it breaks out. For the circle is perfect and infinite in its nature; but it is fixed for ever in its size; it can never be larger or smaller. But the cross, though it has at its heart a collision and a contradiction, can extend its four arms for ever without altering its shape. Because it has a paradox in its centre it can grow without changing. The circle returns upon itself and is bound. The cross opens its arms to the four winds; it is a signpost for free travellers.

---

18. Centripetal force is the force REQUIRED for circular motion. Centrifugal force is the force that makes something flee from the center.

Symbols alone are of even a cloudy value in speaking of this deep matter; and another symbol from physical nature will express sufficiently well the real place of mysticism before mankind. The one created thing which we cannot look at is the one thing in the light of which we look at everything. Like the sun at noonday, mysticism explains everything else by the blaze of its own victorious invisibility. Detached intellectualism is (in the exact sense of a popular phrase) all moonshine; for it is light without heat, and it is secondary light, reflected from a dead world. But the Greeks were right when they made Apollo the god both of imagination and of sanity; for he was both the patron of poetry and the patron of healing. Of necessary dogmas and a special creed I shall speak later. But that transcendentalism[19] by which all men live has primarily much the position of the sun in the sky. We are conscious of it as of a kind of splendid confusion; it is something both shining and shapeless, at once a blaze and a blur. But the circle of the moon is as clear and unmistakable, as recurrent and inevitable, as the circle of Euclid[20] on a blackboard. For the moon is utterly reasonable; and the moon is the mother of lunatics and has given to them all her name.

---

19. Transcendentalists advocated the idea of a personal knowledge of God, believing that no intermediary was needed for spiritual insight. They embraced idealism, focusing on nature and opposing materialism.

20. Sometimes called Euclid of Alexandria to distinguish him from Euclid of Megara, was a Greek mathematician, often referred to as the "founder of geometry" or the "father of geometry".

The Ethics of Elfland

Orthodoxy (**1908**)

"Because children have abounding vitality, because they are in spirit fierce and free, therefore they want things repeated and unchanged. They always say, 'Do it again'; and the grown-up person does it again until he is nearly dead. For grown-up people are not strong enough to exult in monotony. But perhaps God is strong enough to exult in monotony. It is possible that God says every morning, 'Do it again' to the sun; and every evening, 'Do it again' to the moon."

I'M NOT GOING to claim to fully comprehend this entire chapter, but it's one of my favorites if not only for the beautiful passage quoted above about God exulting in monotony like a child.

This chapter is also from *Orthodoxy,* and in it Chesterton is challenging all of our preconceptions about the Universe—the things we take for granted and call "laws" because they repeat. We take for granted that at some point the sun might not set or apples not be red. We don't know why things are what they are, and simply observing repetition makes us no more wise.

I think one thing that makes this chapter hard is that Chesterton is not trying to educate us, he is trying to de-educate us. We are not used to being taught to untangle the knots of what we have been taught. Chesterton is trying to show us the mystery and the unknown that is right in front of our face—everyday wonders that we treat as common. Seeing the world like this is the basis of his philosophy. That if this world is a story, there must be a story teller. It is our bad habit of taking it all for granted that imprisons us in a wonderless world explained away by men in spectacles.

WHEN THE BUSINESS MAN rebukes the idealism of his office-boy, it is commonly in some such speech as this: "Ah, yes, when one is young, one has these ideals in the abstract and these castles in the air; but in middle age they all break up like clouds, and one comes down to a belief in practical politics, to using the machinery one has and getting on with the world as it is." Thus, at least, venerable and philanthropic old men now in their honoured graves used to talk to me when I was a boy.

But since then I have grown up and have discovered that these philanthropic old men were telling lies. What has really happened is exactly the opposite of what they said would happen. They said that I should lose my ideals and begin to believe in the methods of practical politicians. Now, I have not lost my ideals in the least; my faith in fundamentals is exactly what it always was. What I have lost is my old childlike faith in practical politics. I am still as much concerned as ever about the Battle of Armageddon; but I am not so much concerned about the General Election. As a babe I leapt up on my mother's knee at the mere mention of it. No; the vision is always solid and reliable. The vision is always a fact. It is the reality that is often a fraud. As much as I ever did, more than I ever did, I believe in Liberalism. But there was a rosy time of innocence when I believed in Liberals.

I take this instance of one of the enduring faiths because, having now to trace the roots of my personal speculation, this may be counted, I think, as the only positive bias. I was brought up a Liberal, and have always believed in democracy, in the elementary liberal doctrine of a self-governing humanity. If any one finds the phrase vague or threadbare, I can only pause for a moment to explain that the principle of democracy, as I mean it, can be stated in two propositions. The first is this: that the things common to all men are more important than the things peculiar to any men. Ordinary things are more valuable than extraordinary things; nay, they are more extraordinary. Man is something more awful than men; something more strange. The sense of the miracle of humanity itself should be always more vivid to us than any marvels of power, intellect, art, or civilization. The mere man on two legs, as such, should be felt as something more heartbreaking than any music and more startling than any caricature. Death is more tragic even than death by starvation. Having a nose is more comic even than having a Norman nose[1].

This is the first principle of democracy: that the essential things in men are the things they hold in common, not the things they hold separately. And the second principle is merely this: that the political instinct or desire is one of these things which they hold in common. Falling in love is more poetical than dropping into poetry. The democratic contention is that government (helping to rule the tribe) is a thing like falling in love, and not a thing like dropping into poetry. It is not something analogous to playing the church organ, painting on vellum, discovering the North Pole (that insidious habit), looping the loop, being Astronomer Royal, and so on.

For these things we do not wish a man to do at all unless he does them well. It is, on the contrary, a thing analogous to writing one's own love-letters or blowing one's own nose. These things we want a man to do for himself, even if he does them badly. I am not here arguing the truth of any of these conceptions; I know that some moderns are asking to have their wives chosen by scientists, and they may soon be asking, for all I know, to have their noses

---

1. An aquiline nose (also called a Roman nose or hook nose) is a human nose with a prominent bridge, giving it the appearance of being curved or slightly bent. The word aquiline comes from the Latin word aquilinus ("eagle-like"), an allusion to the curved beak of an eagle.

blown by nurses. I merely say that mankind does recognize these universal human functions, and that democracy classes government among them. In short, the democratic faith is this: that the most terribly important things must be left to ordinary men themselves—the mating of the sexes, the rearing of the young, the laws of the state. This is democracy; and in this I have always believed.

But there is one thing that I have never from my youth up been able to understand. I have never been able to understand where people got the idea that democracy was in some way opposed to tradition. It is obvious that tradition is only democracy extended through time. It is trusting to a consensus of common human voices rather than to some isolated or arbitrary record. The man who quotes some German historian against the tradition of the Catholic Church, for instance, is strictly appealing to aristocracy. He is appealing to the superiority of one expert against the awful authority of a mob.

It is quite easy to see why a legend is treated, and ought to be treated, more respectfully than a book of history. The legend is generally made by the majority of people in the village, who are sane. The book is generally written by the one man in the village who is mad. Those who urge against tradition that men in the past were ignorant may go and urge it at the Carlton Club, along with the statement that voters in the slums are ignorant. It will not do for us. If we attach great importance to the opinion of ordinary men in great unanimity when we are dealing with daily matters, there is no reason why we should disregard it when we are dealing with history or fable. Tradition may be defined as an extension of the franchise.

Tradition means giving votes to the most obscure of all classes, our ancestors. It is the democracy of the dead. Tradition refuses to submit to the small and arrogant oligarchy of those who merely happen to be walking about. All democrats object to men being disqualified by the accident of birth; tradition objects to their being disqualified by the accident of death. Democracy tells us not to neglect a good man's opinion, even if he is our groom; tradition asks us not to neglect a good man's opinion, even if he is our father. I, at any rate, cannot separate the two ideas of democracy and tradition; it seems evident to me that they are the same idea. We will have the dead at our councils. The ancient Greeks voted by stones; these shall vote by tombstones. It is all quite regular and official, for most tombstones, like most ballot papers, are marked with a cross.

I have first to say, therefore, that if I have had a bias, it was always a bias in favour of democracy, and therefore of tradition. Before we come to any theoretic or logical beginnings I am content to allow for that personal equation; I have always been more inclined to believe the ruck of hard-working people than to believe that special and troublesome literary class to which I belong. I prefer even the fancies and prejudices of the people who see life from the inside to the clearest demonstrations of the people who see life from the outside. I would always trust the old wives' fables against the old maids' facts. As long as wit is mother wit it can be as wild as it pleases.

Now, I have to put together a general position, and I pretend to no training in such things. I propose to do it, therefore, by writing down one after another the three or four fundamental ideas which I have found for myself, pretty much in the way that I found them. Then I shall roughly synthesise them, summing up my personal philosophy or natural religion; then I shall describe my startling discovery that the whole thing had been discovered before. It had been discovered by Christianity. But of these profound persuasions which I have to recount in order, the earliest was concerned with this element of popular tradition. And without the foregoing explanation touching tradition and democracy I could hardly make my mental experience clear. As it is, I do not know whether I can make it clear, but I now propose to try.

My first and last philosophy, that which I believe in with unbroken certainty, I learnt in the nursery. I generally learnt it from a nurse; that is, from the solemn and star-appointed priestess at once of democracy and tradition. The things I believed most then, the things I believe most now, are the things called fairy tales. They seem to me to be the entirely reasonable things. They are not fantasies: compared with them other things are fantastic. Compared with them religion and rationalism are both abnormal, though religion is abnormally right and rationalism abnormally wrong.

Fairyland is nothing but the sunny country of common sense. It is not earth that judges heaven, but heaven that judges earth; so for me at least it was not earth that criticised elfland, but elfland that criticised the earth. I knew the magic beanstalk before I had tasted beans; I was sure of the Man in the Moon before I was certain of the moon. This was at one with all popular tradition. Modern minor poets are naturalists, and talk about the bush or the brook; but the singers of the old epics and fables were supernaturalists, and talked about the gods of brook and bush. That is what the moderns mean when they say that the ancients did not "appreciate Nature," because they said that Nature was divine. Old nurses do not tell children about the grass, but about the fairies that dance on the grass; and the old Greeks could not see the trees for the dryads.

But I deal here with what ethic and philosophy come from being fed on fairy tales. If I were describing them in detail I could note many noble and healthy principles that arise from them. There is the chivalrous lesson of "Jack the Giant Killer"; that giants should be killed because they are gigantic. It is a manly mutiny against pride as such. For the rebel is older than all the kingdoms, and the Jacobin has more tradition than the Jacobite. There is the lesson of "Cinderella," which is the same as that of the Magnificat— EXAL-TAVIT HUMILES[2]. There is the great lesson of "Beauty and the Beast"; that a thing must be loved BEFORE it is loveable. There is the terrible allegory of the "Sleeping Beauty," which tells how the human creature was blessed with all birthday gifts, yet cursed with death; and how death also may perhaps be softened to a sleep. But I am not concerned with any of the separate statutes of elfland, but with the whole spirit of its law, which I learnt before I could speak, and shall retain when I cannot write. I am concerned with a certain

2. The Magnificat is a canticle, also known as the Song of Mary, the Canticle of Mary and, in the Byzantine tradition, the Ode of the Theotokos. It is traditionally incorporated into the liturgical services of the Catholic Church, the Eastern Orthodox churches, and the Anglican Communion.

EXALTAVIT HUMILES is part of Luke 1:52, from Mary's Song. "He has brought down rulers from their thrones, but has exalted the humble."

way of looking at life, which was created in me by the fairy tales, but has since been meekly ratified by the mere facts.

It might be stated this way. There are certain sequences or developments (cases of one thing following another), which are, in the true sense of the word, reasonable. They are, in the true sense of the word, necessary. Such are mathematical and merely logical sequences. We in fairyland (who are the most reasonable of all creatures) admit that reason and that necessity. For instance, if the Ugly Sisters are older than Cinderella, it is (in an iron and awful sense) NECESSARY that Cinderella is younger than the Ugly Sisters. There is no getting out of it. Haeckel[3] may talk as much fatalism about that fact as he pleases: it really must be. If Jack is the son of a miller, a miller is the father of Jack. Cold reason decrees it from her awful throne: and we in fairyland submit. If the three brothers all ride horses, there are six animals and eighteen legs involved: that is true rationalism, and fairyland is full of it.

But as I put my head over the hedge of the elves and began to take notice of the natural world, I observed an extraordinary thing. I observed that learned men in spectacles were talking of the actual things that happened— dawn and death and so on—as if THEY were rational and inevitable. They talked as if the fact that trees bear fruit were just as NECESSARY as the fact that two and one trees make three. But it is not. There is an enormous difference by the test of fairyland; which is the test of the imagination. You cannot IMAGINE two and one not making three. But you can easily imagine trees not growing fruit; you can imagine them growing golden candlesticks or tigers hanging on by the tail.

These men in spectacles spoke much of a man named Newton, who was hit by an apple, and who discovered a law. But they could not be got to see the distinction between a true law, a law of reason, and the mere fact of apples falling. If the apple hit Newton's nose, Newton's nose hit the apple. That is a true necessity: because we cannot conceive the one occurring without the

---

3. If you have been following the footnotes you already know about Haeckel but if you need a refresher he was an evolutionist, he believed in scientific racism (the idea that racism is biologically justified) and social Darwinism, and by extension determinism (fatalism) the denial of free will - everything we "choose" is a chemical reaction, there is no spirit or soul inside of man controlling him. We are simply reacting.

other. But we can quite well conceive the apple not falling on his nose; we can fancy it flying ardently through the air to hit some other nose, of which it had a more definite dislike. We have always in our fairy tales kept this sharp distinction between the science of mental relations, in which there really are laws, and the science of physical facts, in which there are no laws, but only weird repetitions. We believe in bodily miracles, but not in mental impossibilities. We believe that a Bean-stalk climbed up to Heaven; but that does not at all confuse our convictions on the philosophical question of how many beans make five.

Here is the peculiar perfection of tone and truth in the nursery tales. The man of science says, "Cut the stalk, and the apple will fall"; but he says it calmly, as if the one idea really led up to the other. The witch in the fairy tale says, "Blow the horn, and the ogre's castle will fall"; but she does not say it as if it were something in which the effect obviously arose out of the cause. Doubtless she has given the advice to many champions, and has seen many castles fall, but she does not lose either her wonder or her reason. She does not muddle her head until it imagines a necessary mental connection between a horn and a falling tower. But the scientific men do muddle their heads, until they imagine a necessary mental connection between an apple leaving the tree and an apple reaching the ground. They do really talk as if they had found not only a set of marvellous facts, but a truth connecting those facts. They do talk as if the connection of two strange things physically connected them philosophically. They feel that because one incomprehensible thing constantly follows another incomprehensible thing the two together somehow make up a comprehensible thing. Two black riddles make a white answer.

In fairyland we avoid the word "law"; but in the land of science they are singularly fond of it. Thus they will call some interesting conjecture about how forgotten folks pronounced the alphabet, Grimm's Law[4]. But Grimm's Law is far less intellectual than Grimm's Fairy Tales. The tales are, at any rate, certainly tales; while the law is not a law. A law implies that we know the nature

4. Grimm's law (also known as the First Germanic Sound Shift) is a set of sound laws describing the Proto-Indo-European (PIE) stop consonants as they developed in Proto-Germanic in the 1st millennium BC...or something.

of the generalisation and enactment; not merely that we have noticed some of the effects. If there is a law that pick-pockets shall go to prison, it implies that there is an imaginable mental connection between the idea of prison and the idea of picking pockets. And we know what the idea is. We can say why we take liberty from a man who takes liberties. But we cannot say why an egg can turn into a chicken any more than we can say why a bear could turn into a fairy prince. As IDEAS, the egg and the chicken are further off from each other than the bear and the prince; for no egg in itself suggests a chicken, whereas some princes do suggest bears.

Granted, then, that certain transformations do happen, it is essential that we should regard them in the philosophic manner of fairy tales, not in the unphilosophic manner of science and the "Laws of Nature." When we are asked why eggs turn to birds or fruits fall in autumn, we must answer exactly as the fairy godmother would answer if Cinderella asked her why mice turned to horses or her clothes fell from her at twelve o'clock. We must answer that it is MAGIC. It is not a "law," for we do not understand its general formula. It is not a necessity, for though we can count on it happening practically, we have no right to say that it must always happen. It is no argument for unalterable law (as Huxley fancied) that we count on the ordinary course of things. We do not count on it; we bet on it.

We risk the remote possibility of a miracle as we do that of a poisoned pancake or a world-destroying comet. We leave it out of account, not because it is a miracle, and therefore an impossibility, but because it is a miracle, and therefore an exception. All the terms used in the science books, "law," "necessity," "order," "tendency," and so on, are really unintellectual, because they assume an inner synthesis, which we do not possess. The only words that ever satisfied me as describing Nature are the terms used in the fairy books, "charm," "spell," "enchantment." They express the arbitrariness of the fact and its mystery. A tree grows fruit because it is a MAGIC tree. Water runs downhill because it is bewitched. The sun shines because it is bewitched.

I deny altogether that this is fantastic or even mystical. We may have some mysticism later on; but this fairy-tale language about things is simply rational and agnostic. It is the only way I can express in words my clear and definite perception that one thing is quite distinct from another; that there is no logical connection between flying and laying eggs. It is the man who talks about "a law" that he has never seen who is the mystic. Nay, the ordinary scientific man is strictly a sentimentalist. He is a sentimentalist in this essential sense, that he is soaked and swept away by mere associations. He has so often seen birds fly and lay eggs that he feels as if there must be some dreamy, tender connection between the two ideas, whereas there is none. A forlorn lover might be unable to dissociate the moon from lost love; so the materialist is unable to dissociate the moon from the tide. In both cases there is no connection, except that one has seen them together. A sentimentalist might shed tears at the smell of apple-blossom, because, by a dark association of his own, it reminded him of his boyhood. So the materialist professor (though he conceals his tears) is yet a sentimentalist, because, by a dark association of his own, apple-blossoms remind him of apples. But the cool rationalist from fairyland does not see why, in the abstract, the apple tree should not grow crimson tulips; it sometimes does in his country.

This elementary wonder, however, is not a mere fancy derived from the fairy tales; on the contrary, all the fire of the fairy tales is derived from this. Just as we all like love tales because there is an instinct of sex, we all like astonishing tales because they touch the nerve of the ancient instinct of astonishment. This is proved by the fact that when we are very young children we do not need fairy tales: we only need tales. Mere life is interesting enough. A child of seven is excited by being told that Tommy opened a door and saw a dragon. But a child of three is excited by being told that Tommy opened a door. Boys like romantic tales; but babies like realistic tales—because they find them romantic. In fact, a baby is about the only person, I should think, to whom a modern realistic novel could be read without boring him.

This proves that even nursery tales only echo an almost pre-natal leap of interest and amazement. These tales say that apples were golden only to refresh the forgotten moment when we found that they were green. They make rivers run with wine only to make us remember, for one wild moment, that they run with water. I have said that this is wholly reasonable and even agnostic. And, indeed, on this point I am all for the higher agnosticism; its better name is Ignorance. We have all read in scientific books, and, indeed, in all romances, the story of the man who has forgotten his name. This man walks about the streets and can see and appreciate everything; only he cannot remember who he is. Well, every man is that man in the story. Every man has forgotten who he is. One may understand the cosmos, but never the ego; the self is more distant than any star. Thou shalt love the Lord thy God; but thou shalt not know thyself. We are all under the same mental calamity; we have all forgotten our names. We have all forgotten what we really are. All that we call common sense and rationality and practicality and positivism only means that for certain dead levels of our life we forget that we have forgotten. All that we call spirit and art and ecstasy only means that for one awful instant we remember that we forget.

But though (like the man without memory in the novel) we walk the streets with a sort of half-witted admiration, still it is admiration. It is admiration in English and not only admiration in Latin. The wonder has a positive element of praise. This is the next milestone to be definitely marked on our road through fairyland. I shall speak in the next chapter about optimists and pessimists in their intellectual aspect, so far as they have one. Here I am only trying to describe the enormous emotions which cannot be described. And the strongest emotion was that life was as precious as it was puzzling. It was an ecstasy because it was an adventure; it was an adventure because it was an opportunity. The goodness of the fairy tale was not affected by the fact that there might be more dragons than princesses; it was good to be in a fairy tale. The test of all happiness is gratitude; and I felt grateful, though I hardly knew to whom. Children are grateful when Santa Claus puts in their stockings gifts of toys or sweets. Could I not be grateful to Santa Claus when he put in my stockings the gift of two miraculous legs? We thank people for birthday presents of cigars and slippers. Can I thank no one for the birthday present of birth?

There were, then, these two first feelings, indefensible and indisputable. The world was a shock, but it was not merely shocking; existence was a surprise, but it was a pleasant surprise. In fact, all my first views were exactly uttered in a riddle that stuck in my brain from boyhood. The question was, "What did the first frog say?" And the answer was, "Lord, how you made me jump!" That says succinctly all that I am saying. God made the frog jump;

but the frog prefers jumping. But when these things are settled there enters the second great principle of the fairy philosophy.

Any one can see it who will simply read "Grimm's Fairy Tales" or the fine collections of Mr. Andrew Lang[5]. For the pleasure of pedantry I will call it the Doctrine of Conditional Joy. Touchstone[6] talked of much virtue in an "if"; according to elfin ethics all virtue is in an "if." The note of the fairy utterance always is, "You may live in a palace of gold and sapphire, if you do not say the word "cow"; or "You may live happily with the King's daughter, if you do not show her an onion." The vision always hangs upon a veto. All the dizzy and colossal things conceded depend upon one small thing withheld. All the wild and whirling things that are let loose depend upon one thing that is forbidden. Mr. W.B.Yeats, in his exquisite and piercing elfin poetry, describes the elves as lawless; they plunge in innocent anarchy on the unbridled horses of the air—

"Ride on the crest of the dishevelled tide, And dance upon the mountains like a flame."

It is a dreadful thing to say that Mr. W.B.Yeats does not understand fairyland. But I do say it. He is an ironical Irishman, full of intellectual reactions. He is not stupid enough to understand fairyland. Fairies prefer people of the yokel type like myself; people who gape and grin and do as they are told. Mr. Yeats reads into elfland all the righteous insurrection of his own race. But the lawlessness of Ireland is a Christian lawlessness, founded on reason and justice. The Fenian [7]is rebelling against something he understands only

---

5. Andrew Lang was a Scottish poet, novelist, literary critic, and contributor to the field of anthropology. He is best known as a collector of folk and fairy tales.

6. Touchstone seems to be a fictional character in Shakespeare's play As You Like It. Touchstone is the court jester of Duke Frederick the usurper's court. Throughout the play he comments on the other characters and thus contributes to a better understanding of the play. ...either that or there was another person named Touchstone Chesterton is referring to who I cannot find anything about on Google.

7. A member of a 19th-century revolutionary nationalist organization among the Irish in the US and Ireland. The Fenians staged an unsuccessful revolt in Ireland in 1867 and were responsible for isolated revolutionary acts against the British until the early 20th century, when they were gradually eclipsed by the IRA.

too well; but the true citizen of fairyland is obeying something that he does not understand at all. In the fairy tale an incomprehensible happiness rests upon an incomprehensible condition. A box is opened, and all evils fly out. A word is forgotten, and cities perish. A lamp is lit, and love flies away. A flower is plucked, and human lives are forfeited. An apple is eaten, and the hope of God is gone.

This is the tone of fairy tales, and it is certainly not lawlessness or even liberty, though men under a mean modern tyranny may think it liberty by comparison. People out of Portland Gaol might think Fleet Street[8] free; but closer study will prove that both fairies and journalists are the slaves of duty. Fairy godmothers seem at least as strict as other godmothers. Cinderella received a coach out of Wonderland and a coachman out of nowhere, but she received a command—which might have come out of Brixton—that she should be back by twelve. Also, she had a glass slipper; and it cannot be a coincidence that glass is so common a substance in folk-lore. This princess lives in a glass castle, that princess on a glass hill; this one sees all things in a mirror; they may all live in glass houses if they will not throw stones. For this thin glitter of glass everywhere is the expression of the fact that the happiness is bright but brittle, like the substance most easily smashed by a housemaid or a cat. And this fairy-tale sentiment also sank into me and became my sentiment towards the whole world. I felt and feel that life itself is as bright as the diamond, but as brittle as the window-pane; and when the heavens were compared to the terrible crystal I can remember a shudder. I was afraid that God would drop the cosmos with a crash.

Remember, however, that to be breakable is not the same as to be perishable. Strike a glass, and it will not endure an instant; simply do not strike

---

8. HM Prison Portland is a male Adult/Young Offenders Institution in the village of The Grove on the Isle of Portland, in Dorset, England. It is operated by Her Majesty's Prison Service. The prison was originally opened in 1848 as an adult convict establishment, before becoming a Borstal in 1921, and a YOI in 1988. In 2011 it became an Adult/Young Offenders establishment.

Fleet Street is a major street mostly in the City of London. It runs west to east from Temple Bar at the boundary with the City of Westminster to Ludgate Circus at the site of the London Wall and the River Fleet from which the street was named. The street became known for printing and publishing at the start of the 16th century, and it became the dominant trade so that by the 20th century most British national newspapers operated from here.

it, and it will endure a thousand years. Such, it seemed, was the joy of man, either in elfland or on earth; the happiness depended on NOT DOING SOMETHING which you could at any moment do and which, very often, it was not obvious why you should not do. Now, the point here is that to ME this did not seem unjust. If the miller's third son said to the fairy, "Explain why I must not stand on my head in the fairy palace," the other might fairly reply, "Well, if it comes to that, explain the fairy palace." If Cinderella says, "How is it that I must leave the ball at twelve?" her godmother might answer, "How is it that you are going there till twelve?" If I leave a man in my will ten talking elephants and a hundred winged horses, he cannot complain if the conditions partake of the slight eccentricity of the gift. He must not look a winged horse in the mouth. And it seemed to me that existence was itself so very eccentric a legacy that I could not complain of not understanding the limitations of the vision when I did not understand the vision they limited. The frame was no stranger than the picture. The veto might well be as wild as the vision; it might be as startling as the sun, as elusive as the waters, as fantastic and terrible as the towering trees.

For this reason (we may call it the fairy godmother philosophy) I never could join the young men of my time in feeling what they called the general sentiment of REVOLT. I should have resisted, let us hope, any rules that were evil, and with these and their definition I shall deal in another chapter. But I did not feel disposed to resist any rule merely because it was mysterious. Estates are sometimes held by foolish forms, the breaking of a stick or the payment of a peppercorn: I was willing to hold the huge estate of earth and heaven by any such feudal fantasy. It could not well be wilder than the fact that I was allowed to hold it at all.

At this stage I give only one ethical instance to show my meaning. I could never mix in the common murmur of that rising generation against monogamy, because no restriction on sex seemed so odd and unexpected as sex itself. To be allowed, like Endymion[9], to make love to the moon and then

---

9. Endymion was a handsome shepherd-prince loved by the moon-goddess Selene. When Zeus offered him his choice of destinies, Endymion chose immortality and youth in eternal slumber. He was laid out in a cave on Mount Latmus in Karia (Caria) where his lunar lover would visit him each night.

to complain that Jupiter kept his own moons in a harem seemed to me (bred on fairy tales like Endymion's) a vulgar anti-climax. Keeping to one woman is a small price for so much as seeing one woman. To complain that I could only be married once was like complaining that I had only been born once. It was incommensurate with the terrible excitement of which one was talking. It showed, not an exaggerated sensibility to sex, but a curious insensibility to it. A man is a fool who complains that he cannot enter Eden by five gates at once. Polygamy is a lack of the realization of sex; it is like a man plucking five pears in mere absence of mind.

The aesthetes touched the last insane limits of language in their eulogy on lovely things. The thistledown made them weep; a burnished beetle brought them to their knees. Yet their emotion never impressed me for an instant, for this reason, that it never occurred to them to pay for their pleasure in any sort of symbolic sacrifice. Men (I felt) might fast forty days for the sake of hearing a blackbird sing. Men might go through fire to find a cowslip[10]. Yet these lovers of beauty could not even keep sober for the blackbird. They would not go through common Christian marriage by way of recompense to the cowslip. Surely one might pay for extraordinary joy in ordinary morals. Oscar Wilde said that sunsets were not valued because we could not pay for sunsets. But Oscar Wilde was wrong; we can pay for sunsets. We can pay for them by not being Oscar Wilde.

Well, I left the fairy tales lying on the floor of the nursery, and I have not found any books so sensible since. I left the nurse guardian of tradition and democracy, and I have not found any modern type so sanely radical or so sanely conservative. But the matter for important comment was here: that when I first went out into the mental atmosphere of the modern world, I found that the modern world was positively opposed on two points to my nurse and to the nursery tales. It has taken me a long time to find out that the modern world is wrong and my nurse was right. The really curious thing was this: that modern thought contradicted this basic creed of my boyhood on its two most essential doctrines. I have explained that the fairy tales founded in

---

10. Hey I didn't know this. A cowslip is a common flower apparently.

me two convictions; first, that this world is a wild and startling place, which might have been quite different, but which is quite delightful; second, that before this wildness and delight one may well be modest and submit to the queerest limitations of so queer a kindness. But I found the whole modern world running like a high tide against both my tendernesses; and the shock of that collision created two sudden and spontaneous sentiments, which I have had ever since and which, crude as they were, have since hardened into convictions.

First, I found the whole modern world talking scientific fatalism; saying that everything is as it must always have been, being unfolded without fault from the beginning. The leaf on the tree is green because it could never have been anything else. Now, the fairy-tale philosopher is glad that the leaf is green precisely because it might have been scarlet. He feels as if it had turned green an instant before he looked at it. He is pleased that snow is white on the strictly reasonable ground that it might have been black. Every colour has in it a bold quality as of choice; the red of garden roses is not only decisive but dramatic, like suddenly spilt blood. He feels that something has been DONE. But the great determinists of the nineteenth century were strongly against this native feeling that something had happened an instant before. In fact, according to them, nothing ever really had happened since the beginning of the world. Nothing ever had happened since existence had happened; and even about the date of that they were not very sure.

The modern world as I found it was solid for modern Calvinism, for the necessity of things being as they are. But when I came to ask them I found they had really no proof of this unavoidable repetition in things except the fact that the things were repeated. Now, the mere repetition made the things to me rather more weird than more rational. It was as if, having seen a curiously shaped nose in the street and dismissed it as an accident, I had then seen six other noses of the same astonishing shape. I should have fancied for a moment that it must be some local secret society. So one elephant having a trunk was odd; but all elephants having trunks looked like a plot. I speak here only of an emotion, and of an emotion at once stubborn and subtle. But the repetition in Nature seemed sometimes to be an excited repetition, like that of an angry schoolmaster saying the same thing over and over again. The grass seemed signalling to me with all its fingers at once; the crowded stars seemed bent upon being understood. The sun would make me see him if he rose a thousand times. The recurrences of the universe rose to the maddening rhythm of an incantation, and I began to see an idea.

All the towering materialism which dominates the modern mind rests ultimately upon one assumption; a false assumption. It is supposed that if a thing goes on repeating itself it is probably dead; a piece of clockwork. People feel that if the universe was personal it would vary; if the sun were alive it would dance. This is a fallacy even in relation to known fact. For the variation in human affairs is generally brought into them, not by life, but by death; by the dying down or breaking off of their strength or desire. A man varies his movements because of some slight element of failure or fatigue. He gets into an omnibus because he is tired of walking; or he walks because he is tired of sitting still. But if his life and joy were so gigantic that he never tired of going to Islington, he might go to Islington as regularly as the Thames goes to Sheerness. The very speed and ecstasy of his life would have the stillness of death.

The sun rises every morning. I do not rise every morning; but the variation is due not to my activity, but to my inaction. Now, to put the matter in a popular phrase, it might be true that the sun rises regularly because he never gets tired of rising. His routine might be due, not to a lifelessness, but to a rush of life. The thing I mean can be seen, for instance, in children, when they find some game or joke that they specially enjoy. A child kicks his legs rhythmically through excess, not absence, of life. Because children have abounding vitality, because they are in spirit fierce and free, therefore they want things repeated and unchanged. They always say, "Do it again"; and the grown-up person does it again until he is nearly dead. For grown-up people are not strong enough to exult in monotony. But perhaps God is strong enough to exult in monotony. It is possible that God says every morning, "Do it again" to the sun; and every evening, "Do it again" to the moon. It may not be automatic necessity that makes all daisies alike; it may be that God makes every daisy separately, but has never got tired of making them. It may be that He has the eternal appetite of infancy; for we have sinned and grown old, and our Father is younger than we.

The repetition in Nature may not be a mere recurrence; it may be a theatrical ENCORE. Heaven may ENCORE the bird who laid an egg. If the human being conceives and brings forth a human child instead of bringing forth a fish, or a bat, or a griffin, the reason may not be that we are fixed in an animal fate without life or purpose. It may be that our little tragedy has touched the gods, that they admire it from their starry galleries, and that at the end of every human drama man is called again and again before the curtain. Repetition may go on for millions of years, by mere choice, and at any instant it may stop. Man may stand on the earth generation after generation, and yet each birth be his positively last appearance.

This was my first conviction; made by the shock of my childish emotions meeting the modern creed in mid-career. I had always vaguely felt facts to be miracles in the sense that they are wonderful: now I began to think them miracles in the stricter sense that they were WILFUL. I mean that they were, or might be, repeated exercises of some will. In short, I had always believed that the world involved magic: now I thought that perhaps it involved a magician. And this pointed a profound emotion always present and sub-conscious; that this world of ours has some purpose; and if there is a purpose, there is a person. I had always felt life first as a story: and if there is a story there is a story-teller.

But modern thought also hit my second human tradition. It went against the fairy feeling about strict limits and conditions. The one thing it loved to talk about was expansion and largeness. Herbert Spencer[11] would have been greatly annoyed if any one had called him an imperialist, and therefore it is highly regrettable that nobody did. But he was an imperialist of the lowest type. He popularized this contemptible notion that the size of the solar system ought to over-awe the spiritual dogma of man. Why should a man surrender

---

11. Herbert Spencer was an English philosopher, biologist, anthropologist, and sociologist famous for his hypothesis of social Darwinism whereby superior physical force shapes history.

his dignity to the solar system any more than to a whale? If mere size proves that man is not the image of God, then a whale may be the image of God; a somewhat formless image; what one might call an impressionist portrait.

It is quite futile to argue that man is small compared to the cosmos; for man was always small compared to the nearest tree. But Herbert Spencer, in his headlong imperialism, would insist that we had in some way been conquered and annexed by the astronomical universe. He spoke about men and their ideals exactly as the most insolent Unionist talks about the Irish and their ideals. He turned mankind into a small nationality. And his evil influence can be seen even in the most spirited and honourable of later scientific authors; notably in the early romances of Mr. H.G.Wells. Many moralists have in an exaggerated way represented the earth as wicked. But Mr. Wells and his school made the heavens wicked. We should lift up our eyes to the stars from whence would come our ruin.

But the expansion of which I speak was much more evil than all this. I have remarked that the materialist, like the madman, is in prison; in the prison of one thought. These people seemed to think it singularly inspiring to keep on saying that the prison was very large. The size of this scientific universe gave one no novelty, no relief. The cosmos went on for ever, but not in its wildest constellation could there be anything really interesting; anything, for instance, such as forgiveness or free will. The grandeur or infinity of the secret of its cosmos added nothing to it. It was like telling a prisoner in Reading gaol[12] that he would be glad to hear that the gaol now covered half the county. The warder would have nothing to show the man except more and more long corridors of stone lit by ghastly lights and empty of all that is human. So these expanders of the universe had nothing to show us except more and more infinite corridors of space lit by ghastly suns and empty of all that is divine.

In fairyland there had been a real law; a law that could be broken, for the definition of a law is something that can be broken. But the machinery of this

---

12. Really weird spelling of JAIL.

cosmic prison was something that could not be broken; for we ourselves were only a part of its machinery. We were either unable to do things or we were destined to do them. The idea of the mystical condition quite disappeared; one can neither have the firmness of keeping laws nor the fun of breaking them. The largeness of this universe had nothing of that freshness and airy outbreak which we have praised in the universe of the poet. This modern universe is literally an empire; that is, it was vast, but it is not free. One went into larger and larger windowless rooms, rooms big with Babylonian perspective; but one never found the smallest window or a whisper of outer air.

Their infernal parallels seemed to expand with distance; but for me all good things come to a point, swords for instance. So finding the boast of the big cosmos so unsatisfactory to my emotions I began to argue about it a little; and I soon found that the whole attitude was even shallower than could have been expected. According to these people the cosmos was one thing since it had one unbroken rule. Only (they would say) while it is one thing, it is also the only thing there is. Why, then, should one worry particularly to call it large? There is nothing to compare it with. It would be just as sensible to call it small. A man may say, "I like this vast cosmos, with its throng of stars and its crowd of varied creatures." But if it comes to that why should not a man say, "I like this cosy little cosmos, with its decent number of stars and as neat a provision of live stock as I wish to see"? One is as good as the other; they are both mere sentiments. It is mere sentiment to rejoice that the sun is larger than the earth; it is quite as sane a sentiment to rejoice that the sun is no larger than it is. A man chooses to have an emotion about the largeness of the world; why should he not choose to have an emotion about its smallness?

It happened that I had that emotion. When one is fond of anything one addresses it by diminutives, even if it is an elephant or a life-guardsman. The reason is, that anything, however huge, that can be conceived of as complete, can be conceived of as small. If military moustaches did not suggest a sword or tusks a tail, then the object would be vast because it would be immeasurable. But the moment you can imagine a guardsman you can imagine a small guardsman. The moment you really see an elephant you can call it "Tiny." If you can make a statue of a thing you can make a statuette of it. These people professed that the universe was one coherent thing; but they were not fond of the universe. But I was frightfully fond of the universe and wanted to address it by a diminutive. I often did so; and it never seemed to mind.

Actually and in truth I did feel that these dim dogmas of vitality were better expressed by calling the world small than by calling it large. For about infinity there was a sort of carelessness which was the reverse of the fierce and pious care which I felt touching the pricelessness and the peril of life. They showed only a dreary waste; but I felt a sort of sacred thrift. For economy is far more romantic than extravagance. To them stars were an unending income of halfpence; but I felt about the golden sun and the silver moon as a schoolboy feels if he has one sovereign and one shilling.

These subconscious convictions are best hit off by the colour and tone of certain tales. Thus I have said that stories of magic alone can express my sense that life is not only a pleasure but a kind of eccentric privilege. I may express this other feeling of cosmic cosiness by allusion to another book always read in boyhood, "Robinson Crusoe," which I read about this time, and which owes its eternal vivacity to the fact that it celebrates the poetry of limits, nay, even the wild romance of prudence. Crusoe is a man on a small rock with a few comforts just snatched from the sea: the best thing in the book is simply the list of things saved from the wreck. The greatest of poems is an inventory. Every kitchen tool becomes ideal because Crusoe might have dropped it in the sea. It is a good exercise, in empty or ugly hours of the day, to look at anything, the coal-scuttle or the book-case, and think how happy one could be to have brought it out of the sinking ship on to the solitary island. But it is a better exercise still to remember how all things have had this hair-breadth escape: everything has been saved from a wreck. Every man has had one horrible adventure: as a hidden untimely birth he had not been, as infants that never see the light. Men spoke much in my boyhood of restricted or ruined men of genius: and it was common to say that many a man was a Great Might-Have-Been. To me it is a more solid and startling fact that any man in the street is a Great Might-Not-Have-Been.

But I really felt (the fancy may seem foolish) as if all the order and number of things were the romantic remnant of Crusoe's ship. That there are two sexes and one sun, was like the fact that there were two guns and one axe. It was poignantly urgent that none should be lost; but somehow, it was rather fun that none could be added. The trees and the planets seemed like things saved from the wreck: and when I saw the Matterhorn I was glad that it had not been overlooked in the confusion. I felt economical about the stars as if they were sapphires (they are called so in Milton's Eden): I hoarded the hills. For the universe is a single jewel, and while it is a natural cant to talk of a jewel as peerless and priceless, of this jewel it is literally true. This cosmos is indeed without peer and without price: for there cannot be another one.

Thus ends, in unavoidable inadequacy, the attempt to utter the unutterable things. These are my ultimate attitudes towards life; the soils for the seeds of doctrine. These in some dark way I thought before I could write, and felt before I could think: that we may proceed more easily afterwards, I will roughly recapitulate them now. I felt in my bones; first, that this world does not explain itself. It may be a miracle with a supernatural explanation; it may be a conjuring trick, with a natural explanation. But the explanation of the conjuring trick, if it is to satisfy me, will have to be better than the natural explanations I have heard. The thing is magic, true or false. Second, I came to feel as if magic must have a meaning, and meaning must have some one to mean it. There was something personal in the world, as in a work of art; whatever it meant it meant violently. Third, I thought this purpose beautiful in its old design, in spite of its defects, such as dragons. Fourth, that the proper form of thanks to it is some form of humility and restraint: we should thank God for beer and Burgundy by not drinking too much of them. We owed, also, an obedience to whatever made us. And last, and strangest, there had come into my mind a vague and vast impression that in some way all good was a remnant to be stored and held sacred out of some primordial ruin. Man had saved his good as Crusoe saved his goods: he had saved them from a wreck. All this I felt and the age gave me no encouragement to feel it. And all this time I had not even thought of Christian theology.

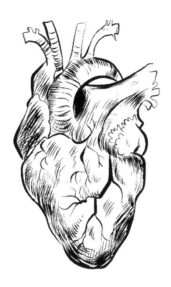

The Paradoxes of Christianity

Orthodoxy (**1908**)

"There never was anything so perilous or so exciting as orthodoxy. It was sanity: and to be sane is more dramatic than to be mad."

LET ME FIRST SAY that this is not one of the easier Chesterton chapters to read. It is full of historical references that fly over the head of an uneducated man such as myself. I did my best to footnote all the historical references made in this chapter, hopefully with some minor degree of accuracy and helpfulness.

But the concept of the Paradox is a common Chestertonian theme, so I thought it was an important introductory essay for the Chestertonian noob. He makes many fascinating points in this chapter. You may not get them all, as I have failed to. But there is enough here to get you thinking about the Christian faith in ways you probably never have before.

At the heart of it, I think Chesterton's love of the paradox is that in Christianity, there is no *one* virtue that is made dominant. Unlike most religions that lean heavily in the way of mercy or vengeance, health or pleasure, Christianity equally and fully holds all of it. I find this all the more important as we live in a particularly vengeful time when mercilessness is en vogue. Christianity sees the sin fully, it sees evil in all its seemingly endless darkness, recognizing the massive debt to be paid, and yet it also sees mercy and love shining bright and burning eternal to cast out every shadow no matter how black.

THE REAL TROUBLE with this world of ours is not that it is an unreasonable world, nor even that it is a reasonable one. The commonest kind of trouble is that it is nearly reasonable, but not quite. Life is not an illogicality; yet it is a trap for logicians. It looks just a little more mathematical and regular than it is; its exactitude is obvious, but its inexactitude is hidden; its wildness lies in wait. I give one coarse instance of what I mean. Suppose some mathematical creature from the moon were to reckon up the human body; he would at once see that the essential thing about it was that it was duplicate. A man is two men, he on the right exactly resembling him on the left. Having noted that there was an arm on the right and one on the left, a leg on the right and one on the left, he might go further and still find on each side the same number of fingers, the same number of toes, twin eyes, twin ears, twin nostrils, and even twin lobes of the brain. At last he would take it as a law; and then, where he found a heart on one side, would deduce that there was another heart on the other. And just then, where he most felt he was right, he would be wrong.

It is this silent swerving from accuracy by an inch that is the uncanny element in everything. It seems a sort of secret treason in the universe. An apple or an orange is round enough to get itself called round, and yet is not round after all. The earth itself is shaped like an orange in order to lure some simple astronomer into calling it a globe. A blade of grass is called after the blade of a sword, because it comes to a point; but it doesn't. Everywhere in things there is this element of the quiet and incalculable. It escapes the rationalists, but it never escapes till the last moment. From the grand curve of our earth it could easily be inferred that every inch of it was thus curved. It would seem rational that as a man has a brain on both sides, he should have a heart on both sides. Yet scientific men are still organizing expeditions to find the North Pole[1], because they are so fond of flat country. Scientific men are also still organizing expeditions to find a man's heart; and when they try to find it, they generally get on the wrong side of him.

Now, actual insight or inspiration is best tested by whether it guesses these hidden malformations or surprises. If our mathematician from the moon saw the two arms and the two ears, he might deduce the two shoulder-blades and the two halves of the brain. But if he guessed that the man's heart was in the right place, then I should call him something more than a mathematician. Now, this is exactly the claim which I have since come to propound for Christianity. Not merely that it deduces logical truths, but that when it suddenly becomes illogical, it has found, so to speak, an illogical truth. It not only goes right about things, but it goes wrong (if one may say so) exactly where the things go wrong. Its plan suits the secret irregularities, and expects the unexpected. It is simple about the simple truth; but it is stubborn about the subtle truth. It will admit that a man has two hands, it will not admit (though all the Modernists wail to it) the obvious deduction that he has two hearts. It is my only purpose in this chapter to point this out; to show that whenever we feel there is something odd in Christian theology, we shall generally find that there is something odd in the truth.

I have alluded to an unmeaning phrase to the effect that such and such a creed cannot be believed in our age. Of course, anything can be believed

1. The North Pole had not yet been reached when GK wrote this book. That would happen about four years later.

in any age. But, oddly enough, there really is a sense in which a creed, if it is believed at all, can be believed more fixedly in a complex society than in a simple one. If a man finds Christianity true in Birmingham, he has actually clearer reasons for faith than if he had found it true in Mercia.[2] For the more complicated seems the coincidence, the less it can be a coincidence. If snowflakes fell in the shape, say, of the heart of Midlothian[3], it might be an accident. But if snowflakes fell in the exact shape of the maze at Hampton Court, I think one might call it a miracle.

It is exactly as of such a miracle that I have since come to feel of the philosophy of Christianity. The complication of our modern world proves the truth of the creed more perfectly than any of the plain problems of the ages of faith. It was in Notting Hill and Battersea that I began to see that Christianity was true. This is why the faith has that elaboration of doctrines and details which so much distresses those who admire Christianity without believing in it. When once one believes in a creed, one is proud of its complexity, as scientists are proud of the complexity of science. It shows how rich it is in discoveries. If it is right at all, it is a compliment to say that it's elaborately right. A stick might fit a hole or a stone a hollow by accident. But a key and a lock are both complex. And if a key fits a lock, you know it is the right key.

But this involved accuracy of the thing makes it very difficult to do what I now have to do, to describe this accumulation of truth. It is very hard for a man to defend anything of which he is entirely convinced. It is comparatively easy when he is only partially convinced. He is partially convinced because he has found this or that proof of the thing, and he can expound it. But a man is not really convinced of a philosophic theory when he finds that something proves it. He is only really convinced when he finds that everything proves it. And the more converging reasons he finds pointing to this conviction, the more bewildered he is if asked suddenly to sum them up.

---

2. Mercia was an ancient region of England that bordered Wales—was pagan, then became Christian in 656, which was astonishingly close to the time of Christ.

3. The Heart of Mid-Lothian is a mosaic in the pavement outside of St. Giles Cathedral in Edinborough.

Thus, if one asked an ordinary intelligent man, on the spur of the moment, "Why do you prefer civilization to savagery?" he would look wildly round at object after object, and would only be able to answer vaguely, "Why, there is that bookcase . . . and the coals in the coal-scuttle . . . and pianos . . . and policemen." The whole case for civilization is that the case for it is complex. It has done so many things. But that very multiplicity of proof which ought to make reply overwhelming makes reply impossible.

There is, therefore, about all complete conviction a kind of huge helpless-ness. The belief is so big that it takes a long time to get it into action. And this hesitation chiefly arises, oddly enough, from an indifference about where one should begin. All roads lead to Rome; which is one reason why many people never get there. In the case of this defence of the Christian conviction I confess that I would as soon begin the argument with one thing as another; I would begin it with a turnip or a taximeter cab. But if I am to be at all careful about making my meaning clear, it will, I think, be wiser to continue the current arguments of the last chapter[4], which was concerned to urge the first of these mystical coincidences, or rather ratifications.

All I had hitherto heard of Christian theology had alienated me from it. I was a pagan at the age of twelve, and a complete agnostic by the age of sixteen; and I cannot understand any one passing the age of seventeen without having asked himself so simple a question. I did, indeed, retain a cloudy reverence for a cosmic deity and a great historical interest in the Founder of Christian-ity. But I certainly regarded Him as a man; though perhaps I thought that, even in that point, He had an advantage over some of His modern critics.

I read the scientific and sceptical literature of my time—all of it, at least, that I could find written in English and lying about; and I read nothing else; I mean I read nothing else on any other note of philosophy. The penny dreadfuls[5] which I also read were indeed in a healthy and heroic tradition of

4. The previous chapter he is referring to is The Flag of the World, in which Chesterton attempts to convey the idea that we all are born with this idea about the world, that it was created good, and that there is good-ness to be sought, even though there is no evidence of that. (that's my messy interpretation).

5. Cheap popular serial literature produced during the 19th century in the United Kingdom.

Christianity; but I did not know this at the time. I never read a line of Christian apologetics. I read as little as I can of them now. It was Huxley and Herbert Spencer and Bradlaugh[6] who brought me back to orthodox theology. They sowed in my mind my first wild doubts of doubt. Our grandmothers were quite right when they said that Tom Paine and the free-thinkers[7] unsettled the mind. They do. They unsettled mine horribly. The rationalist made me question whether reason was of any use whatever; and when I had finished Herbert Spencer I had got as far as doubting (for the first time) whether evolution had occurred at all. As I laid down the last of Colonel Ingersoll's[8] atheistic lectures the dreadful thought broke across my mind, "Almost thou persuadest me to be a Christian." I was in a desperate way.

This odd effect of the great agnostics in arousing doubts deeper than their own might be illustrated in many ways. I take only one. As I read and re-read all the non-Christian or anti-Christian accounts of the faith, from Huxley to Bradlaugh, a slow and awful impression grew gradually but graphically upon my mind—the impression that Christianity must be a most extraordinary thing. For not only (as I understood) had Christianity the most flaming vices, but it had apparently a mystical talent for combining vices which seemed inconsistent with each other. It was attacked on all sides and for all contradictory reasons. No sooner had one rationalist demonstrated that it was too far to the east than another demonstrated with equal clearness that it was much too far to the west. No sooner had my indignation died down at its angular and aggressive squareness than I was called up again to notice and condemn its enervating and sensual roundness. In case any reader has not come across the thing I mean, I will give such instances as I remember at random of this self-contradiction in the sceptical attack. I give four or five of them; there are fifty more.

---

6. Sir Julian Huxley, Herbert Spencer, and Charles Bradlaugh — All leading atheist/evolutionist intellectuals of Chesterton's day.

7. Paine's critique of institutionalized religion and advocacy of rational thinking influenced many of the leading self-proclaimed "freethinkers" in the 19th and 20th centuries. Buncha neck beards.

8. An American lawyer, writer, and orator during the Golden Age of Free Thought, who campaigned in defense of agnosticism. He was nicknamed "The Great Agnostic".

Thus, for instance, I was much moved by the eloquent attack on Christianity as a thing of inhuman gloom; for I thought (and still think) sincere pessimism the unpardonable sin. Insincere pessimism is a social accomplishment, rather agreeable than otherwise; and fortunately nearly all pessimism is insincere. But if Christianity was, as these people said, a thing purely pessimistic and opposed to life, then I was quite prepared to blow up St. Paul's Cathedral. But the extraordinary thing is this. They did prove to me in Chapter I. (to my complete satisfaction) that Christianity was too pessimistic; and then, in Chapter II., they began to prove to me that it was a great deal too optimistic.

One accusation against Christianity was that it prevented men, by morbid tears and terrors, from seeking joy and liberty in the bosom of Nature. But another accusation was that it comforted men with a fictitious providence, and put them in a pink-and-white nursery. One great agnostic asked why Nature was not beautiful enough, and why it was hard to be free. Another great agnostic objected that Christian optimism, "the garment of make-believe woven by pious hands," hid from us the fact that Nature was ugly, and that it was impossible to be free. One rationalist had hardly done calling Christianity a nightmare before another began to call it a fool's paradise.

This puzzled me; the charges seemed inconsistent. Christianity could not at once be the black mask on a white world, and also the white mask on a black world. The state of the Christian could not be at once so comfortable that he was a coward to cling to it, and so uncomfortable that he was a fool to stand it. If it falsified human vision it must falsify it one way or another; it could not wear both green and rose-coloured spectacles. I rolled on my tongue with a terrible joy, as did all young men of that time, the taunts which Swinburne[9] hurled at the dreariness of the creed—

---

9. Swinburne is referenced often in Chesterton's work. He was a decadent playwright and poet who often gloated about the many vices and deviancies he engaged in, including homosexuality and beastiality, though people seemed to think it was all for show (he is said to have spread a rumour that he had had sex with, then eaten, a monkey). He wrote about many taboo topics, such as lesbianism, cannibalism, sadomasochism, and anti-theism. Guy sounds like a hoot!

"Thou hast conquered, O pale Galilaean, the world has grown gray with Thy breath." [10]

But when I read the same poet's accounts of paganism (as in "Atalanta"), I gathered that the world was, if possible, more gray before the Galilean breathed on it than afterwards. The poet maintained, indeed, in the abstract, that life itself was pitch dark. And yet, somehow, Christianity had darkened it. The very man who denounced Christianity for pessimism was himself a pessimist. I thought there must be something wrong. And it did for one wild moment cross my mind that, perhaps, those might not be the very best judges of the relation of religion to happiness who, by their own account, had neither one nor the other.

It must be understood that I did not conclude hastily that the accusations were false or the accusers fools. I simply deduced that Christianity must be something even weirder and wickeder than they made out. A thing might have these two opposite vices; but it must be a rather queer thing if it did. A man might be too fat in one place and too thin in another; but he would be an odd shape. At this point my thoughts were only of the odd shape of the Christian religion; I did not allege any odd shape in the rationalistic mind.

Here is another case of the same kind. I felt that a strong case against Christianity lay in the charge that there is something timid, monkish, and unmanly about all that is called "Christian," especially in its attitude towards resistance and fighting. The great sceptics of the nineteenth century were largely virile. Bradlaugh in an expansive way, Huxley, in a reticent way, were decidedly men. In comparison, it did seem tenable that there was something weak and over patient about Christian counsels. The Gospel paradox about the other cheek, the fact that priests never fought, a hundred things made plausible the accusation that Christianity was an attempt to make a man too

---

10. This line is from Swinburne's "Hymn to Proserpine" -- The poem is addressed to the goddess Proserpina, the Roman equivalent of Persephone (Persephone was the daughter of Zeus and Demeter. She became the queen of the underworld after her abduction by Hades, the god of the underworld, with the approval of her father, Zeus) but laments the rise of Christianity for displacing the pagan goddess and her pantheon.

like a sheep. I read it and believed it, and if I had read nothing different, I should have gone on believing it. But I read something very different.

I turned the next page in my agnostic manual, and my brain turned upside down. Now I found that I was to hate Christianity not for fighting too little, but for fighting too much. Christianity, it seemed, was the mother of wars. Christianity had deluged the world with blood. I had got thoroughly angry with the Christian, because he never was angry. And now I was told to be angry with him because his anger had been the most huge and horrible thing in human history; because his anger had soaked the earth and smoked to the sun. The very people who reproached Christianity with the meekness and non-resistance of the monasteries were the very people who reproached it also with the violence and valour of the Crusades. It was the fault of poor old Christianity (somehow or other) both that Edward the Confessor did not fight and that Richard Coeur de Leon did[11]. The Quakers (we were told) were the only characteristic Christians; and yet the massacres of Cromwell and Alva[12] were characteristic Christian crimes. What could it all mean? What was this Christianity which always forbade war and always produced wars? What could be the nature of the thing which one could abuse first because it would not fight, and second because it was always fighting? In what world of riddles was born this monstrous murder and this monstrous meekness? The shape of Christianity grew a queerer shape every instant.

---

11. Edward the Confessor was known for his image of a feeble old king preparing his soul for heaven. He was known as a holy king who worked miracles. Later, his image was reshaped by medieval monks, reinventing him as a 'Confessor' (a saint who 'confessed' the faith by virtuous living). Edward came to be seen as an otherworldly king, more interested in preparing his soul for heaven than in governing England.

Richard Coeur De Leon was King of England from 1189 until his death in 1199. Richard is known as Richard Cœur de Lion or Richard the Lionheart because of his reputation as a great military leader and warrior.

12. Oliver Cromwell was an English general and statesman who, first as a subordinate and later as Commander-in-Chief, led armies of the Parliament of England against King Charles I during the English Civil War, subsequently ruling the British Isles as Lord Protector from 1653 until his death in 1658. He acted simultaneously as head of state and head of government of the new republican commonwealth. As a ruler, he executed an aggressive and effective foreign policy. Nevertheless, Cromwell's policy of religious toleration for Protestant denominations during the Protectorate extended only to "God's peculiar", and not to those considered by him to be heretics, such as the Quakers, Socinians, and Ranters. He carried out the Drogheda massacre where thousands were killed including many civilians.

The Spanish King's captain-general Alva, also known as the Iron Duke, was a key figures behind the Spanish Fury (or the Spanish Terror) — a number of violent sackings of cities in the Low Countries mostly by Spanish Habsburg armies, that occurred in the years 1572–1579 during the Dutch Revolt. In some cases the sack did not follow the taking of a city. In others the sack was ordered, or at least not restrained, by Spanish commanders after the fall of a city.

I take a third case; the strangest of all, because it involves the one real objection to the faith. The one real objection to the Christian religion is simply that it is one religion. The world is a big place, full of very different kinds of people. Christianity (it may reasonably be said) is one thing confined to one kind of people; it began in Palestine, it has practically stopped with Europe. I was duly impressed with this argument in my youth, and I was much drawn towards the doctrine often preached in Ethical Societies— I mean the doctrine that there is one great unconscious church of all humanity founded on the omnipresence of the human conscience.

Creeds, it was said, divided men; but at least morals united them. The soul might seek the strangest and most remote lands and ages and still find essential ethical common sense. It might find Confucius under Eastern trees, and he would be writing "Thou shalt not steal." It might decipher the darkest hieroglyphic on the most primeval desert, and the meaning when deciphered would be "Little boys should tell the truth." I believed this doctrine of the brotherhood of all men in the possession of a moral sense, and I believe it still—with other things. And I was thoroughly annoyed with Christianity for suggesting (as I supposed) that whole ages and empires of men had utterly escaped this light of justice and reason.

But then I found an astonishing thing. I found that the very people who said that mankind was one church from Plato to Emerson were the very people who said that morality had changed altogether, and that what was right in one age was wrong in another. If I asked, say, for an altar, I was told that we needed none, for men our brothers gave us clear oracles and one creed in their universal customs and ideals. But if I mildly pointed out that one of men's universal customs was to have an altar, then my agnostic teachers turned clean round and told me that men had always been in darkness and the superstitions of savages.

I found it was their daily taunt against Christianity that it was the light of one people and had left all others to die in the dark. But I also found that it was their special boast for themselves that science and progress were the discovery of one people, and that all other peoples had died in the dark. Their chief insult to Christianity was actually their chief compliment to themselves, and there seemed to be a strange unfairness about all their relative insistence on the two things. When considering some pagan or agnostic, we were to remember that all men had one religion; when considering some mystic or spiritualist, we were only to consider what absurd religions some men had. We could trust the ethics of Epictetus[13], because ethics had never changed. We must not trust the ethics of Bossuet[14], because ethics had changed. They changed in two hundred years, but not in two thousand.

This began to be alarming. It looked not so much as if Christianity was bad enough to include any vices, but rather as if any stick was good enough to beat Christianity with. What again could this astonishing thing be like which people were so anxious to contradict, that in doing so they did not mind contradicting themselves? I saw the same thing on every side. I can give no further space to this discussion of it in detail; but lest any one supposes that I have unfairly selected three accidental cases I will run briefly through a few others.

Thus, certain sceptics wrote that the great crime of Christianity had been its attack on the family; it had dragged women to the loneliness and contemplation of the cloister, away from their homes and their children. But, then, other sceptics (slightly more advanced) said that the great crime of Christianity was forcing the family and marriage upon us; that it doomed women to the drudgery of their homes and children, and forbade them loneliness and contemplation. The charge was actually reversed. Or, again, certain phrases in the Epistles or the marriage service, were said by the anti-Christians to show contempt for woman's intellect. But I found that the anti-Christians themselves had a contempt for woman's intellect; for it was their great sneer

---

13. Epictetus was a Greek Stoic philosopher. His teachings were written down and published by his pupil Arrian in his Discourses and Enchiridion. Epictetus taught that philosophy is a way of life and not just a theoretical discipline. To Epictetus, all external events are beyond our control; we should accept whatever happens calmly and dispassionately. However, individuals are responsible for their own actions, which they can examine and control through rigorous self-discipline.

14. Jacques-Bénigne Lignel Bossuet was a French bishop and theologian, renowned for his sermons and other addresses. He has been considered by many to be one of the most brilliant orators of all time and a masterly French stylist.

at the Church on the Continent that "only women" went to it. Or again, Christianity was reproached with its naked and hungry habits; with its sackcloth and dried peas. But the next minute Christianity was being reproached with its pomp and its ritualism; its shrines of porphyry[15] and its robes of gold. It was abused for being too plain and for being too coloured. Again Christianity had always been accused of restraining sexuality too much, when Bradlaugh the Malthusian[16] discovered that it restrained it too little. It is often accused in the same breath of prim respectability and of religious extravagance. Between the covers of the same atheistic pamphlet I have found the faith rebuked for its disunion, "One thinks one thing, and one another," and rebuked also for its union, "It is difference of opinion that prevents the world from going to the dogs." In the same conversation a free-thinker, a friend of mine, blamed Christianity for despising Jews, and then despised it himself for being Jewish.

I wished to be quite fair then, and I wish to be quite fair now; and I did not conclude that the attack on Christianity was all wrong. I only concluded that if Christianity was wrong, it was very wrong indeed. Such hostile horrors might be combined in one thing, but that thing must be very strange and solitary. There are men who are misers, and also spendthrifts; but they are rare. There are men sensual and also ascetic; but they are rare. But if this mass of mad contradictions really existed, quakerish and bloodthirsty, too gorgeous and too thread-bare, austere, yet pandering preposterously to the lust of the eye, the enemy of women and their foolish refuge, a solemn pessimist and a silly optimist, if this evil existed, then there was in this evil something quite supreme and unique.

---

15. A hard igneous rock containing crystals, usually of feldspar, in a fine-grained, typically reddish ground-mass.

16. A Malthusian is one who subcribes to the views on population put forth by Thomas Robert Malthus — an English cleric, scholar and influential economist in the fields of political economy and demography.

The short version of Mathus's theory is that an increase in a nation's food production improved the well-being of the population, but the improvement was temporary because it led to population growth, which in turn restored the original per capita production level. In other words, humans had a propensity to utilize abundance for population growth rather than for maintaining a high standard of living, a view that has become known as the "Malthusian trap" or the "Malthusian spectre".

Malthus saw population growth as being inevitable whenever conditions improved, thereby precluding real progress towards a utopian society.

For I found in my rationalist teachers no explanation of such exceptional corruption. Christianity (theoretically speaking) was in their eyes only one of the ordinary myths and errors of mortals. THEY gave me no key to this twisted and unnatural badness. Such a paradox of evil rose to the stature of the supernatural. It was, indeed, almost as supernatural as the infallibility of the Pope. An historic institution, which never went right, is really quite as much of a miracle as an institution that cannot go wrong. The only explanation which immediately occurred to my mind was that Christianity did not come from heaven, but from hell. Really, if Jesus of Nazareth was not Christ, He must have been Antichrist.

And then in a quiet hour a strange thought struck me like a still thunderbolt. There had suddenly come into my mind another explanation. Suppose we heard an unknown man spoken of by many men. Suppose we were puzzled to hear that some men said he was too tall and some too short; some objected to his fatness, some lamented his leanness; some thought him too dark, and some too fair. One explanation (as has been already admitted) would be that he might be an odd shape. But there is another explanation. He might be the right shape. Outrageously tall men might feel him to be short. Very short men might feel him to be tall. Old bucks who are growing stout might consider him insufficiently filled out; old beaux who were growing thin might feel that he expanded beyond the narrow lines of elegance. Perhaps Swedes (who have pale hair like tow) called him a dark man, while negroes considered him distinctly blonde.

Perhaps (in short) this extraordinary thing is really the ordinary thing; at least the normal thing, the centre. Perhaps, after all, it is Christianity that is sane and all its critics that are mad—in various ways. I tested this idea by asking myself whether there was about any of the accusers anything morbid that might explain the accusation. I was startled to find that this key fitted a lock. For instance, it was certainly odd that the modern world charged Christianity at once with bodily austerity and with artistic pomp. But then it was also odd, very odd, that the modern world itself combined extreme bodily luxury with an extreme absence of artistic pomp. The modern man thought Becket's[17] robes too rich and his meals too poor. But then the modern man was really exceptional in history; no man before ever ate such elaborate dinners in such ugly clothes. The modern man found the church too simple exactly where modern life is too complex; he found the church too gorgeous exactly where modern life is too dingy. The man who disliked the plain fasts and feasts was mad on entrees. The man who disliked vestments wore a pair of preposterous trousers. And surely if there was any insanity involved in the matter at all it was in the trousers, not in the simply falling robe. If there was any insanity at all, it was in the extravagant entrees, not in the bread and wine.

I went over all the cases, and I found the key fitted so far. The fact that Swinburne was irritated at the unhappiness of Christians and yet more irritated at their happiness was easily explained. It was no longer a complication of diseases in Christianity, but a complication of diseases in Swinburne. The restraints of Christians saddened him simply because he was more hedonist than a healthy man should be. The faith of Christians angered him because he was more pessimist than a healthy man should be. In the same way the Malthusians by instinct attacked Christianity; not because there is anything especially anti-Malthusian about Christianity, but because there is something a little anti-human about Malthusianism.

Nevertheless it could not, I felt, be quite true that Christianity was merely sensible and stood in the middle. There was really an element in it of emphasis and even frenzy which had justified the secularists in their superficial criticism. It might be wise, I began more and more to think that it was wise, but it was not merely worldly wise; it was not merely temperate and respectable. Its fierce crusaders and meek saints might balance each other; still, the crusaders were very fierce and the saints were very meek, meek beyond all decency.

Now, it was just at this point of the speculation that I remembered my thoughts about the martyr and the suicide. In that matter there had been this combination between two almost insane positions which yet somehow

17. Thomas Becket was Archbishop of Canterbury from 1162 until his murder in 1170. He is venerated as a saint and martyr by both the Catholic Church and the Anglican Communion. He engaged in conflict with Henry II, King of England, over the rights and privileges of the Church and was murdered by followers of the king in Canterbury Cathedral. Soon after his death, he was canonised by Pope Alexander III.

amounted to sanity. This was just such another contradiction; and this I had already found to be true. This was exactly one of the paradoxes in which sceptics found the creed wrong; and in this I had found it right. Madly as Christians might love the martyr or hate the suicide, they never felt these passions more madly than I had felt them long before I dreamed of Christianity. Then the most difficult and interesting part of the mental process opened, and I began to trace this idea darkly through all the enormous thoughts of our theology. The idea was that which I had outlined touching the optimist and the pessimist; that we want not an amalgam or compromise, but both things at the top of their energy; love and wrath both burning. Here I shall only trace it in relation to ethics. But I need not remind the reader that the idea of this combination is indeed central in orthodox theology. For orthodox theology has specially insisted that Christ was not a being apart from God and man, like an elf, nor yet a being half human and half not, like a centaur, but both things at once and both things thoroughly, very man and very God. Now let me trace this notion as I found it.

All sane men can see that sanity is some kind of equilibrium; that one may be mad and eat too much, or mad and eat too little. Some moderns have indeed appeared with vague versions of progress and evolution which seeks to destroy the MESON[18] or balance of Aristotle. They seem to suggest that we are meant to starve progressively, or to go on eating larger and larger breakfasts every morning for ever. But the great truism of the MESON remains for all thinking men, and these people have not upset any balance except their own. But granted that we have all to keep a balance, the real interest comes in with the question of how that balance can be kept. That was the problem which

---

18. Aristotle theorized that virtue was the mean (MESON) between two extremes. In his work *Nicomachean Ethics* Aristotle says: "In everything that is continuous and divisible it is possible to take more, less, or an equal amount, and that either in terms of the thing itself or relatively to us; and the equal is an intermediate between excess and defect. By the intermediate in the object I mean that which is equidistant from each of the extremes, which is one and the same for all men; by the intermediate relatively to us that which is neither too much nor too little- and this is not one, nor the same for all. For instance, if ten is many and two is few, six is the intermediate, taken in terms of the object; for it exceeds and is exceeded by an equal amount; this is intermediate according to arithmetical proportion. But the intermediate relatively to us is not to be taken so; if ten pounds are too much for a particular person to eat and two too little, it does not follow that the trainer will order six pounds; for this also is perhaps too much for the person who is to take it, or too little- too little for Milo, too much for the beginner in athletic exercises. The same is true of running and wrestling. Thus a master of any art avoids excess and defect, but seeks the intermediate and chooses this- the intermediate not in the object but relatively to us."

Paganism tried to solve: that was the problem which I think Christianity solved and solved in a very strange way.

Paganism declared that virtue was in a balance; Christianity declared it was in a conflict: the collision of two passions apparently opposite. Of course they were not really inconsistent; but they were such that it was hard to hold simultaneously. Let us follow for a moment the clue of the martyr and the suicide; and take the case of courage. No quality has ever so much addled the brains and tangled the definitions of merely rational sages. Courage is almost a contradiction in terms. It means a strong desire to live taking the form of a readiness to die. "He that will lose his life, the same shall save it," is not a piece of mysticism for saints and heroes. It is a piece of everyday advice for sailors or mountaineers. It might be printed in an Alpine guide or a drill book. This paradox is the whole principle of courage; even of quite earthly or quite brutal courage. A man cut off by the sea may save his life if he will risk it on the precipice.

He can only get away from death by continually stepping within an inch of it. A soldier surrounded by enemies, if he is to cut his way out, needs to combine a strong desire for living with a strange carelessness about dying. He must not merely cling to life, for then he will be a coward, and will not escape. He must not merely wait for death, for then he will be a suicide, and will not escape. He must seek his life in a spirit of furious indifference to it; he must desire life like water and yet drink death like wine. No philosopher, I fancy, has ever expressed this romantic riddle with adequate lucidity, and I certainly have not done so. But Christianity has done more: it has marked the limits of it in the awful graves of the suicide and the hero, showing the distance between him who dies for the sake of living and him who dies for the sake of dying. And it has held up ever since above the European lances the banner of the mystery of chivalry: the Christian courage, which is a disdain of death; not the Chinese courage, which is a disdain of life[19].

---

19. Boom! China roasted.

And now I began to find that this duplex passion was the Christian key to ethics everywhere. Everywhere the creed made a moderation out of the still crash of two impetuous emotions. Take, for instance, the matter of modesty, of the balance between mere pride and mere prostration. The average pagan, like the average agnostic, would merely say that he was content with himself, but not insolently self-satisfied, that there were many better and many worse, that his deserts were limited, but he would see that he got them. In short, he would walk with his head in the air; but not necessarily with his nose in the air. This is a manly and rational position, but it is open to the objection we noted against the compromise between optimism and pessimism—the "resignation" of Matthew Arnold[20]. Being a mixture of two things, it is a dilution of two things; neither is present in its full strength or contributes its full colour. This proper pride does not lift the heart like the tongue of trumpets; you cannot go clad in crimson and gold for this. On the other hand, this mild rationalist modesty does not cleanse the soul with fire and make it clear like crystal; it does not (like a strict and searching humility) make a man as a little child, who can sit at the feet of the grass[21]. It does not make him look up and see marvels; for Alice must grow small if she is to be Alice in Wonderland. Thus it loses both the poetry of being proud and the

---

20. Resignation is a poem by Matthew Arnold who was a poet in Chesterton's time. Chesterton called him "the most serious man alive," which is not exactly a compliment coming from Chesterton. Here is the final stanza of that poem (which is easily Googlable) for some context if you are at all able to understand poems. I am not.

Enough, we live:—and if a life,
  With large results so little rife,
  Though bearable, seen hardly worth
  This pomp of worlds, this pain of birth;
  Yet, Fausta, the mute turf we tread,
  The solemn hills around us spread,
  This stream that falls incessantly,
  The strange-scrawl'd rocks, the lonely sky,
  If I might lend their life a voice,
  Seem to bear rather than rejoice.
  And even could the intemperate prayer
  Man iterates, while these forbear,
  For movement, for an ampler sphere,
  Pierce Fate's impenetrable ear;
  Not milder is the general lot
  Because our spirits have forgot,
  In action's dizzying eddy whirl'd,
  The something that infects the world.

21. Hey, direct reference to Tremendous Trifles right here.

poetry of being humble. Christianity sought by this same strange expedient to save both of them.

It separated the two ideas and then exaggerated them both. In one way Man was to be haughtier than he had ever been before; in another way he was to be humbler than he had ever been before. In so far as I am Man I am the chief of creatures. In so far as I am a man I am the chief of sinners. All humility that had meant pessimism, that had meant man taking a vague or mean view of his whole destiny—all that was to go. We were to hear no more the wail of Ecclesiastes that humanity had no pre-eminence over the brute, or the awful cry of Homer that man was only the saddest of all the beasts of the field[22]. Man was a statue of God walking about the garden. Man had pre-eminence over all the brutes; man was only sad because he was not a beast, but a broken god.

The Greek had spoken of men creeping on the earth, as if clinging to it. Now Man was to tread on the earth as if to subdue it. Christianity thus held a thought of the dignity of man that could only be expressed in crowns rayed like the sun and fans of peacock plumage. Yet at the same time it could hold a thought about the abject smallness of man that could only be expressed in fasting and fantastic submission, in the gray ashes of St. Dominic and the white snows of St. Bernard[23]. When one came to think of ONE'S SELF, there was vista and void enough for any amount of bleak abnegation and bitter truth. There the realistic gentleman could let himself go—as long as he let himself go at himself. There was an open playground for the happy pessimist. Let him say anything against himself short of blaspheming the original aim

22. The actual quote from Homer's Odyssey — well not actual because it's translated to English — is: "Of all creatures that breathe and move upon the earth, nothing is bred that is weaker than man."

23. In my 15 minute deep dive on these two saints I must admit I could not find any link between either of them and ashes or snow. St. Dominic is the very same guy who the Dominican Republic is named after. As for St. Bernard... the main one I looked up, I found nothing. But there is this other guy who the dog is named after:

The dog name "St. Bernard" originates from the Great St Bernard Hospice, a traveler's hospice on the often treacherous Great St Bernard Pass in the Western Alps, between Switzerland and Italy.The pass, the lodge, and the dogs are named for Bernard of Menthon, the 11th century Italian monk who established the station.

So there is some snow of St. Bernard. Hmph. Well, anyway, both were very disciplined and ascetic. Sorry, not a great footnote but then again, at least this Chesterton book HAS footnotes. I tried!

of his being; let him call himself a fool and even a damned fool (though that is Calvinistic); but he must not say that fools are not worth saving. He must not say that a man, QUA[24] man, can be valueless. Here, again in short, Christianity got over the difficulty of combining furious opposites, by keeping them both, and keeping them both furious. The Church was positive on both points. One can hardly think too little of one's self. One can hardly think too much of one's soul.

Take another case: the complicated question of charity, which some highly uncharitable idealists seem to think quite easy. Charity is a paradox, like modesty and courage. Stated baldly, charity certainly means one of two things—pardoning unpardonable acts, or loving unlovable people. But if we ask ourselves (as we did in the case of pride) what a sensible pagan would feel about such a subject, we shall probably be beginning at the bottom of it. A sensible pagan would say that there were some people one could forgive, and some one couldn't: a slave who stole wine could be laughed at; a slave who betrayed his benefactor could be killed, and cursed even after he was killed. In so far as the act was pardonable, the man was pardonable. That again is rational, and even refreshing; but it is a dilution. It leaves no place for a pure horror of injustice, such as that which is a great beauty in the innocent. And it leaves no place for a mere tenderness for men as men, such as is the whole fascination of the charitable.

Christianity came in here as before. It came in startlingly with a sword, and clove one thing from another. It divided the crime from the criminal. The criminal we must forgive unto seventy times seven. The crime we must not forgive at all. It was not enough that slaves who stole wine inspired partly anger and partly kindness. We must be much more angry with theft than before, and yet much kinder to thieves than before. There was room for wrath and love to run wild. And the more I considered Christianity, the more I found that while it had established a rule and order, the chief aim of that order was to give room for good things to run wild.

---

24. Man qua man is apparently from Ayn Rand, it means — as I saw one explanation — Man as being Man; by his existence and fundamental nature in the deepest metaphysical sense. I'm lost.

Mental and emotional liberty are not so simple as they look. Really they require almost as careful a balance of laws and conditions as do social and political liberty. The ordinary aesthetic anarchist who sets out to feel everything freely gets knotted at last in a paradox that prevents him feeling at all. He breaks away from home limits to follow poetry. But in ceasing to feel home limits he has ceased to feel the "Odyssey." He is free from national prejudices and outside patriotism. But being outside patriotism he is outside "Henry V." Such a literary man is simply outside all literature: he is more of a prisoner than any bigot. For if there is a wall between you and the world, it makes little difference whether you describe yourself as locked in or as locked out.

What we want is not the universality that is outside all normal sentiments; we want the universality that is inside all normal sentiments. It is all the difference between being free from them, as a man is free from a prison, and being free of them as a man is free of a city. I am free from Windsor Castle (that is, I am not forcibly detained there), but I am by no means free of that building. How can man be approximately free of fine emotions, able to swing them in a clear space without breakage or wrong? THIS was the achievement of this Christian paradox of the parallel passions. Granted the primary dogma of the war between divine and diabolic, the revolt and ruin of the world, their optimism and pessimism, as pure poetry, could be loosened like cataracts.

St. Francis, in praising all good, could be a more shouting optimist than Walt Whitman.[25] St. Jerome, in denouncing all evil, could paint the world

---

25. Compare this line from St. Francis's Canticle of the Sun...

Most high, all powerful, all good Lord! All praise is yours, all glory, all honor, and all blessing. To you, alone, Most High, do they belong. ... Be praised, my Lord, through Brothers Wind and Air, and clouds and storms, and all the weather, through which you give your creatures sustenance.

...To Walt Whitman's poem "O Me, Oh Life!" He ends with the line:
The question, O me! so sad, recurring—What good amid these, O me, O life?

And then adds...

Answer.
That you are here—that life exists and identity,
That the powerful play goes on, and you may contribute a verse.

He just gives the answer right there at the end. Not very poemy if you ask me!

blacker than Schopenhauer[26]. Both passions were free because both were kept in their place. The optimist could pour out all the praise he liked on the gay music of the march, the golden trumpets, and the purple banners going into battle. But he must not call the fight needless. The pessimist might draw as darkly as he chose the sickening marches or the sanguine wounds. But he must not call the fight hopeless.

So it was with all the other moral problems, with pride, with protest, and with compassion. By defining its main doctrine, the Church not only kept seemingly inconsistent things side by side, but, what was more, allowed them to break out in a sort of artistic violence otherwise possible only to anarchists. Meekness grew more dramatic than madness. Historic Christianity rose into a high and strange COUP DE THEATRE of morality—things that are to virtue what the crimes of Nero[27] are to vice. The spirits of indignation and of charity took terrible and attractive forms, ranging from that monkish fierceness that

---

26. Arthur Schopenhauer 's view of life is that both individually and as a whole, it is meaningless, primarily because of suffering. He believed it would be better if there was nothing. Given the situation, the best we can do is to extend mercy to our fellow sufferers.

27. Do you want to know the greatest crimes of Nero? Buckle your Chesterbelts!

PERSECUTING CHRISTIANS: He devised elaborate ways to cause horrible suffering to Christians, including crucifying his victims upside down and turning them into human candles for his garden.

MATRICIDE: He first tried to kill his mom using a self-sinking boat. But when that didn't work he just had his guards kill her.

KILLING TWO WIVES: Nero divorced his first wife, Ocatavia, had her banished and then executed, all so he could marry his mistress. Three years later she died too when Nero kicked her in her belly while she was pregnant.

STEALING: Nero went to extreme lengths to squeeze all he could out of the empire. He had the temples raided, the silver currency devalued and there are reports of him forcing the richest people in Rome to leave their properties to him in their wills, before he made them commit suicide.

MURDER: He got his teenage rival killed by having a woman poison his drink at a dinner party.

SEXUAL DEBAUCHERY: Historian Suetonius wrote, "Virtually every part of [Nero's] body had been employed in filthy lusts." He goes on to say that Nero devised a game where he disguised himself in the pelt of a wild animal and attacked the private parts of men and women tied to stakes.

CASTRATION: This one is really messed up. When Nero saw the boy Sporus, he was so struck by how much he looked like his dead wife that he had him castrated and arranged a wedding ceremony, complete with dowry and bridal veil.

That's messed up.

Source: HistoryExtra.com

scourged like a dog the first and greatest of the Plantagenets[28], to the sublime pity of St. Catherine[29], who, in the official shambles, kissed the bloody head of the criminal. Poetry could be acted as well as composed. This heroic and monumental manner in ethics has entirely vanished with supernatural religion. They, being humble, could parade themselves: but we are too proud to be prominent. Our ethical teachers write reasonably for prison reform; but we are not likely to see Mr. Cadbury[30], or any eminent philanthropist, go into Reading Gaol and embrace the strangled corpse before it is cast into the quicklime. Our ethical teachers write mildly against the power of millionaires; but we are not likely to see Mr. Rockefeller[31], or any modern tyrant, publicly whipped in Westminster Abbey.

Thus, the double charges of the secularists, though throwing nothing but darkness and confusion on themselves, throw a real light on the faith. It is true that the historic Church has at once emphasised celibacy and emphasised the family; has at once (if one may put it so) been fiercely for having children

---

28. The Plantagenet dynasty ruled England for over three hundred years, from 1154 -1485, providing England with fourteen of its kings.

The dynasty produced such varied characters as the energetic Henry II, arguably one of England's greatest monarchs and his legendary son, Richard the Lionheart, who led the Third Crusade against Saladin into the Holy Land. The highly aesthetic Henry III and his son, the indomitable Edward I, who conquered Wales and became known as the Hammer of the Scots for his campaigns into that country, where he fought William Wallace and Robert the Bruce, the most famous of Scotland's sons, and Henry V, the conqueror of France, who bequeathed the diadems of both countries to his pious and ineffectual son, Henry VI.

The Plantagenets, described by Bacon as "a race much dipped in their own blood" finally destroyed themselves in the bloody dynastic struggle we know of as the
Wars of the Roses

Source: EnglishMonarchs.co.uk

29. St. Catherine of Siena was said to be able to read the thoughts and know the temptations of her associates, even at long distances. She saw people's secret sins and confronted these people, urging them to repent. She touched hearts so effectively that the Friars Preachers had to designate three priests to handle the confessions of her penitents.

She interceded fiercely for hardened criminals in Siena's jails. Even blasphemous prisoners embraced the gospel when she visited them.

She cared for the sick. It is written that God healed plague victims when she prayed for them or touched them.

30. As previously noted, the Quaker candy magnate known for his cream eggs, who was also known in his time for his philanthropy.

31. John D. Rockefeller monopolized the oil industry through many questionable practices and was seen as bearing some responsibility for the Ludlow massacre in which many innocents including women and children died.

and fiercely for not having children. It has kept them side by side like two strong colours, red and white, like the red and white upon the shield of St. George[32]. It has always had a healthy hatred of pink. It hates that combination of two colours which is the feeble expedient of the philosophers. It hates that evolution of black into white which is tantamount to a dirty gray. In fact, the whole theory of the Church on virginity might be symbolized in the statement that white is a colour: not merely the absence of a colour. All that I am urging here can be expressed by saying that Christianity sought in most of these cases to keep two colours coexistent but pure. It is not a mixture like russet or purple; it is rather like a shot silk[33], for a shot silk is always at right angles, and is in the pattern of the cross.

So it is also, of course, with the contradictory charges of the anti-Christians about submission and slaughter. It IS true that the Church told some men to fight and others not to fight; and it IS true that those who fought were like thunderbolts and those who did not fight were like statues. All this simply means that the Church preferred to use its Supermen and to use its Tolstoyans[34]. There must be SOME good in the life of battle, for so many good men have enjoyed being soldiers. There must be SOME good in the idea of non-resistance, for so many good men seem to enjoy being Quakers. All that the Church did (so far as that goes) was to prevent either of these good things from ousting the other. They existed side by side. The Tolstoyans, having all

---

32. A white shield with a Red Cross which became associated with the Crusades.

33. Shot silk is a fabric which is made up of silk woven from warp and weft yarns of two or more colours producing an iridescent appearance.

34. Tolstoyans identify themselves as Christians, but do not generally belong to an institutional Church. They tend to focus more on following the teachings of Jesus, rather than on his miracles or divinity.

They attempt to live an ascetic and simple life, preferring to be vegetarian, non-smoking, teetotal and chaste. Tolstoyans are considered Christian pacifists and advocate nonresistance in all circumstances.

Tolstoy's understanding of what it means to be Christian was defined by the Sermon on the Mount and summed up in five simple propositions: 1. Love your enemies; 2. Do not be angry; 3. Do not fight evil with evil, but return evil with good; 4. Do not lust; 5. Do not take oaths.

They do not support or participate in the government which they consider immoral, violent and corrupt. Tolstoy rejected the state (as it only exists on the basis of physical force) and all institutions that are derived from it – the police, law courts and army. Thus, many now regard them as Christian anarchists.Historically, Tolstoy's ideas have had some influence on anarchist thought, specifically on anarcho-pacifism.

In short: They were a buncha dirty hippies!

the scruples of monks, simply became monks. The Quakers became a club instead of becoming a sect. Monks said all that Tolstoy says; they poured out lucid lamentations about the cruelty of battles and the vanity of revenge. But the Tolstoyans are not quite right enough to run the whole world; and in the ages of faith they were not allowed to run it. The world did not lose the last charge of Sir James Douglas[35] or the banner of Joan the Maid[36]. And sometimes this pure gentleness and this pure fierceness met and justified their juncture; the paradox of all the prophets was fulfilled, and, in the soul of St. Louis[37], the lion lay down with the lamb. But remember that this text is too lightly interpreted. It is constantly assured, especially in our Tolstoyan tendencies, that when the lion lies down with the lamb the lion becomes lamb-like. But that is brutal annexation and imperialism on the part of the lamb. That is simply the lamb absorbing the lion instead of the lion eating the lamb. The real problem is—Can the lion lie down with the lamb and still retain his royal ferocity? THAT is the problem the Church attempted; THAT is the miracle she achieved.

This is what I have called guessing the hidden eccentricities of life. This is knowing that a man's heart is to the left and not in the middle. This is knowing not only that the earth is round, but knowing exactly where it is flat. Christian doctrine detected the oddities of life. It not only discovered the law, but it foresaw the exceptions. Those underrate Christianity who say that it discovered mercy; any one might discover mercy. In fact every one

---

35. James Douglas, Robert Bruce's indomitable captain during the Wars of Independence. He carried the heart of Bruce in a cask around his neck, which is where the term "Brave Heart" comes from. There is a lot about him to be read but as for his final charge this was written about him:

His end clearly upon him, the story as recounted by Sir Walter Scott goes that Douglas removed the cask from around his neck, declared aloud "Pass first in fight" as thou wert wont to do, and Douglas will follow thee, or die", then charged the enemy one last time.

Source: Castlehunter.scot

36. Joan of Arc's (also known as Joan the Maid) description of her banner at her trial in Rouen: "I had a banner, the field of which was sown with lilies. On it the world was represented [the image of God holding the world] and two angels at the sides. It was of linen or white boucassin. There was written upon it, as it seems to me, these words: Jesus Maria, and it was fringed with silk."

37. Louis IX of France is one of the most notable European monarchs of the Middle Ages. His reign is remembered as a medieval golden age in which the Kingdom of France reached an economic as well as political peak. His fellow European rulers esteemed him highly, not only for his pre-eminence in arms or the unmatched wealth of his kingdom, but also for his reputation of fairness and moral integrity: he was often asked to arbitrate their disputes.

did. But to discover a plan for being merciful and also severe— THAT was to anticipate a strange need of human nature. For no one wants to be forgiven for a big sin as if it were a little one. Any one might say that we should be neither quite miserable nor quite happy. But to find out how far one MAY be quite miserable without making it impossible to be quite happy—that was a discovery in psychology. Any one might say, "Neither swagger nor grovel"; and it would have been a limit. But to say, "Here you can swagger and there you can grovel"—that was an emancipation.

This was the big fact about Christian ethics; the discovery of the new balance. Paganism had been like a pillar of marble, upright because it was proportioned with symmetry. Christianity was like a huge and ragged and romantic rock, which, though it sways on its pedestal at a touch, yet, because its exaggerated excrescences exactly balance each other, is enthroned there for a thousand years. In a Gothic cathedral the columns were all different, but they were all necessary. Every support seemed an accidental and fantastic support; every buttress was a flying buttress. So in Christendom apparent accidents balanced. Becket[38] wore a hair shirt under his gold and crimson, and there is much to be said for the combination; for Becket got the benefit of the hair shirt while the people in the street got the benefit of the crimson and gold. It is at least better than the manner of the modern millionaire, who has the black and the drab outwardly for others, and the gold next his heart.

But the balance was not always in one man's body as in Becket's; the balance was often distributed over the whole body of Christendom. Because a man prayed and fasted on the Northern snows, flowers could be flung at his festival in the Southern cities; and because fanatics drank water on the sands of Syria, men could still drink cider in the orchards of England. This is what makes Christendom at once so much more perplexing and so much more interesting than the Pagan empire; just as Amiens Cathedral is not better but more interesting than the Parthenon.

---

38. After Archbishop Thomas Becket was murdered, his body was stripped of his bloodied vestments. It was found that Becket had been wearing a rough hair shirt that would have caused him considerable discomfort, as would irritation from the lice and maggots that infested the shirt. It was also revealed that Becket subjected himself to whipping up to three times a day, not for any masochistic pleasure but as a form of monastic mortification that was designed to focus the mind on spiritual matters.

If any one wants a modern proof of all this, let him consider the curious fact that, under Christianity, Europe (while remaining a unity) has broken up into individual nations. Patriotism is a perfect example of this deliberate balancing of one emphasis against another emphasis. The instinct of the Pagan empire would have said, "You shall all be Roman citizens, and grow alike; let the German grow less slow and reverent; the Frenchmen less experimental and swift." But the instinct of Christian Europe says, "Let the German remain slow and reverent, that the Frenchman may the more safely be swift and ex- perimental. We will make an equipoise out of these excesses. The absurdity called Germany shall correct the insanity called France."

Last and most important, it is exactly this which explains what is so inexplicable to all the modern critics of the history of Christianity. I mean the monstrous wars about small points of theology, the earthquakes of emo- tion about a gesture or a word. It was only a matter of an inch; but an inch is everything when you are balancing. The Church could not afford to swerve a hair's breadth on some things if she was to continue her great and dar- ing experiment of the irregular equilibrium. Once let one idea become less powerful and some other idea would become too powerful. It was no flock of sheep the Christian shepherd was leading, but a herd of bulls and tigers, of terrible ideals and devouring doctrines, each one of them strong enough to turn to a false religion and lay waste the world.

Remember that the Church went in specifically for dangerous ideas; she was a lion tamer. The idea of birth through a Holy Spirit, of the death of a divine being, of the forgiveness of sins, or the fulfilment of prophecies, are ideas which, any one can see, need but a touch to turn them into something blasphemous or ferocious. The smallest link was let drop by the artificers of the Mediterranean, and the lion of ancestral pessimism burst his chain in the forgotten forests of the north. Of these theological equalisations I have to speak afterwards. Here it is enough to notice that if some small mistake were made in doctrine, huge blunders might be made in human happiness. A sentence phrased wrong about the nature of symbolism would have broken all the best statues in Europe. A slip in the definitions might stop all the dances; might wither all the Christmas trees or break all the Easter eggs. Doctrines had to be defined within strict limits, even in order that man might enjoy general human liberties. The Church had to be careful, if only that the world might be careless.

This is the thrilling romance of Orthodoxy. People have fallen into a foolish habit of speaking of orthodoxy as something heavy, humdrum, and safe. There never was anything so perilous or so exciting as orthodoxy. It was sanity: and to be sane is more dramatic than to be mad. It was the equilibrium of a man behind madly rushing horses, seeming to stoop this way and to sway that, yet in every attitude having the grace of statuary and the accuracy of arithmetic. The Church in its early days went fierce and fast with any war-horse; yet it is utterly unhistoric to say that she merely went mad along one idea, like a vulgar fanaticism. She swerved to left and right, so exactly as to avoid enormous obstacles. She left on one hand the huge bulk of Arianism[39], buttressed by all the worldly powers to make Christianity too worldly. The next instant she was swerving to avoid an orientalism, which would have made it too unworldly.

The orthodox Church never took the tame course or accepted the conventions; the orthodox Church was never respectable. It would have been easier to have accepted the earthly power of the Arians. It would have been easy, in the Calvinistic seventeenth century, to fall into the bottomless pit of predestination. It is easy to be a madman: it is easy to be a heretic. It is always easy to let the age have its head; the difficult thing is to keep one's own. It is always easy to be a modernist; as it is easy to be a snob. To have fallen into any of those open traps of error and exaggeration which fashion after fashion

---

39. Not skinheads, but an influential heresy denying the divinity of Christ, originating with the Alexandrian priest Arius (c. 250– c. 336). Arianism maintained that the Son of God was created by the Father and was therefore neither coeternal with the Father, nor consubstantial.

and sect after sect set along the historic path of Christendom—that would indeed have been simple. It is always simple to fall; there are an infinity of angles at which one falls, only one at which one stands. To have fallen into any one of the fads from Gnosticism[40] to Christian Science[41] would indeed have been obvious and tame. But to have avoided them all has been one whirling adventure; and in my vision the heavenly chariot flies thundering through the ages, the dull heresies sprawling and prostrate, the wild truth reeling but erect.

---

40. A prominent heretical movement of the 2nd-century Christian Church, partly of pre-Christian origin. Gnostic doctrine taught that the world was created and ruled by a lesser divinity, the demiurge, and that Christ was an emissary of the remote supreme divine being, esoteric knowledge (gnosis) of whom enabled the redemption of the human spirit.

41. Christian Science is a set of beliefs and practices belonging to the metaphysical family of new religious movements. It was developed in 19th-century New England by Mary Baker Eddy, who argued in her 1875 book Science and Health that sickness is an illusion that can be corrected by prayer alone.

In short: Neither Christian nor science!

The Drift From Domesticity

The Thing: Why I Am a Catholic, **(1929)**

"Let us say for the sake of simplicity, a fence or gate erected across a road. The more modern type of reformer goes gaily up to it and says, "I don't see the use of this; let us clear it away." To which the more intelligent type of reformer will do well to answer: "If you don't see the use of it, I certainly won't let you clear it away. Go away and think. Then, when you can come back and tell me that you do see the use of it, I may allow you to destroy it."

I PUT THIS chapter in the book mostly because of its first paragraph which contains one of Chesterton's most famous illustrations: Chesterton's Fence. It is also the inspiration for the title of this book which is a play on "Chesterton's Gate," which is technically accurate, because he says "gate" right there in the text.

The chapter itself is a great companion to the chapter on the Institution of the Family. He is answering critics who think the domestic family needs to be broken up, that children should be freed from their parents and educated by the state, and that this would somehow make everyone more free. He argues that this is a stupid position to take, put forth mostly by the ignorance of people who never saw the beauty, freedom, and function of the institution of the family in the first place.

IN THE MATTER of reforming things, as distinct from deforming them, there is one plain and simple principle; a principle which will probably be called a paradox. There exists in such a case a certain institution or law; let us say for the sake of simplicity, a fence or gate erected across a road. The more modern type of reformer goes gaily up to it and says, "I don't see the use of this; let us clear it away." To which the more intelligent type of reformer will do well to answer: "If you don't see the use of it, I certainly won't let you clear it away. Go away and think. Then, when you can come back and tell me that you do see the use of it, I may allow you to destroy it."

This paradox rests on the most elementary common sense. The gate or fence did not grow there. It was not set up by somnambulists[1] who built it in their sleep. It is highly improbable that it was put there by escaped lunatics who were for some reason loose in the street. Some person had some reason for thinking it would be a good thing for somebody. And until we know what the reason was, we really cannot judge whether the reason was reasonable. It is extremely probable that we have overlooked some whole aspect of the question, if something set up by human beings like ourselves seems to be entirely meaningless and mysterious.

There are reformers who get over this difficulty by assuming that all their fathers were fools; but if that be so, we can only say that folly appears to be a hereditary disease. But the truth is that nobody has any business to destroy a social institution until he has really seen it as an historical institution. If he knows how it arose, and what purposes it was supposed to serve, he may really be able to say that they were bad purposes, or that they have since become bad purposes, or that they are purposes which are no longer served. But if

---

1. Fancy pants word for "sleep walkers".

he simply stares at the thing as a senseless monstrosity that has somehow sprung up in his path, it is he and not the traditionalist who is suffering from an illusion. We might even say that he is seeing things in a nightmare.

This principle applies to a thousand things, to trifles as well as true institutions, to convention as well as to conviction. It was exactly the sort of person, like Joan of Arc, who did know why women wore skirts, who was most justified in not wearing one; it was exactly the sort of person, like St. Francis, who did sympathise with the feast and the fireside, who was most entitled to become a beggar on the open road[2]. And when, in the general emancipation of modern society, the Duchess says she does not see why she shouldn't play leapfrog, or the Dean declares that he sees no valid canonical reason why he should not stand on his head, we may say to these persons with patient benevolence: "Defer, therefore, the operation you contemplate until you have realised by ripe reflection what principle or prejudice you are violating. Then play leapfrog and stand on your head and the Lord be with you."

Among the traditions that are being thus attacked, not intelligently but most unintelligently, is the fundamental human creation called the Household or the Home. That is a typical thing which men attack, not because they can see through it, but because they cannot see it at all. They beat at it blindly, in a fashion entirely haphazard and opportunist; and many of them would pull it down without even pausing to ask why it was ever put up. It is true that only a few of them would have avowed this object in so many words. That only proves how very blind and blundering they are. But they have fallen into a habit of mere drift and gradual detachment from family life; something that is often merely accidental and devoid of any definite theory at all.

But though it is accidental it is none the less anarchical. And it is all the more anarchical for not being anarchist. It seems to be largely founded on individual irritation; an irritation which varies with the individual. We are merely told that in this or that case a particular temperament was tormented by a particular environment; but nobody even explained how the evil arose,

2. Sr. Francis was born into a wealthy family to a father who was a successful silk merchant. However he abandoned his affluent lifestyle not long after returning from military service and chose to be homeless.

let alone whether the evil is really escaped. We are told that in this or that family Grandmamma talked a great deal of nonsense, which God knows is true; or that it is very difficult to have intimate intellectual relations with Uncle Gregory without telling him he is a fool, which is indeed the case. But nobody seriously considers the remedy, or even the malady; or whether the existing individualistic dissolution is a remedy at all.

Much of this business began with the influence of Ibsen, a very powerful dramatist and an exceedingly feeble philosopher. I suppose that Nora of THE DOLL'S HOUSE[3] was intended to be an inconsequent person; but certainly her most inconsequent action was her last. She complained that she was not yet fit to look after children, and then proceeded to get as far as possible from the children, that she might study them more closely. There is one simple test and type of this neglect of scientific thinking and the sense of a social rule; the neglect which has now left us with nothing but a welter of exceptions. I have read hundreds and thousands of times, in all the novels and newspapers of our epoch, certain phrases about the just right of the young to liberty, about the unjust claim of the elders to control, about the conception that all souls must be free or all citizens equal, about the absurdity of authority or the degradation of obedience. I am not arguing those matters directly at the moment. But what strikes me as astounding, in a logical sense, is that not one of these myriad novelists and newspaper-men ever seems to think of asking the next and most obvious question.

It never seems to occur to them to enquire what becomes of the opposite obligation. If the child is free from the first to disregard the parent, why is not the parent free from the first to disregard the child? If Mr. Jones, Senior, and Mr. Jones, Junior, are only two free and equal citizens, why should one citizen sponge on another citizen for the first fifteen years of his life? Why should the elder Mr. Jones be expected to feed, clothe and shelter out of his

---

3 The Doll's House is a famous play written by Ibsen, a Norwegian playwright Chesterton mentions often. He seems to admire Ibsen as a writer but not as a philosopher. The play deals with the fate of a married woman, who at the time in Norway lacked reasonable opportunities for self-fulfillment in a male-dominated world, despite the fact that Ibsen denies it was his intent to write a feminist play. It aroused a great sensation at the time, and caused a "storm of outraged controversy" that went beyond the theatre to the world newspapers and society.

own pocket another person who is entirely free of any obligations to him? If the bright young thing cannot be asked to tolerate her grandmother, who has become something of a bore, why should the grandmother or the mother have tolerated the bright young thing at a period of her life when she was by no means bright? Why did they laboriously look after her at a time when her contributions to the conversation were seldom epigrammatic and not often intelligible? Why should Jones Senior stand drinks and free meals to anybody so unpleasant as Jones Junior, especially in the immature phases of his existence? Why should he not throw the baby out of the window; or at any rate, kick the boy out of doors? It is obvious that we are dealing with a real relation, which may be equality, but is certainly not similarity.

Some social reformers try to evade this difficulty, I know, by some vague notions about the State or an abstraction called Education eliminating the parental function. But this, like many notions of solid scientific persons, is a wild illusion of the nature of mere moonshine. It is based on that strange new superstition, the idea of infinite resources of organisation. It is as if officials grew like grass or bred like rabbits. There is supposed to be an endless supply of salaried persons, and of salaries for them; and they are to undertake all that human beings naturally do for themselves; including the care of children. But men cannot live by taking in each other's baby-linen. They cannot provide a tutor for each citizen; who is to tutor the tutors? Men cannot be educated by machinery; and though there might be a Robot bricklayer or scavenger, there will never be a Robot schoolmaster or governess.

The actual effect of this theory is that one harassed person has to look after a hundred children, instead of one normal person looking after a normal number of them. Normally that normal person is urged by a natural force, which costs nothing and does not require a salary; the force of natural affection for his young, which exists even among the animals. If you cut off that natural force, and substitute a paid bureaucracy, you are like a fool who should pay men to turn the wheel of his mill, because he refused to use wind or water which he could get for nothing. You are like a lunatic who should carefully water his garden with a watering-can, while holding up an umbrella to keep off the rain.

It is now necessary to recite these truisms; for only by doing so can we begin to get a glimpse of that REASON for the existence of the family, which I began this essay by demanding.

They were all familiar to our fathers, who believed in the links of kinship and also in the links of logic. To-day our logic consists mostly of missing links; and our family largely of absent members. But, anyhow, this is the right end at which to begin any such enquiry; and not at the tail-end or the fag-end[4] of some private muddle, by which Dick has become discontented or Susan has gone off on her own. If Dick or Susan wish to destroy the family because they do not see the use of it, I say as I said in the beginning; if they do not see the use of it, they had much better preserve it. They have no business even to think of destroying it until they have seen the use of it.

But it has other uses, besides the obvious fact that it means a necessary social work being done for love when it cannot be done for money; and (one might almost dare to hint) presumably to be repaid with love since it is never repaid in money. On that simple side of the matter the general situation is easy to record. The existing and general system of society, subject in our own age and industrial culture to very gross abuses and painful problems, is nevertheless a normal one. It is the idea that the commonwealth is made up of a number of small kingdoms, of which a man and a woman become the king and queen and in which they exercise a reasonable authority, subject to the common sense of the commonwealth, until those under their care grow up to found similar kingdoms and exercise similar authority. This is the social structure of mankind, far older than all its records and more universal than any of its religions; and all attempts to alter it are mere talk and tomfoolery.

But the other advantage of the small group is now not so much neglected as simply not realised. Here again we have some extraordinary delusions

---

4. Whoa. Watch it GK. Canceled!

spread all over the literature and journalism of our time. Those delusions now exist in such a degree that we may say, for all practical purposes, that when a thing has been stated about a thousand times as obviously true, it is almost certain to be obviously false. One such statement may be specially noted here. There is undoubtedly something to be said against domesticity and in favour of the general drift towards life in hotels, clubs, colleges, communal settlements and the rest; or for a social life organized on the plan of the great commercial systems of our time. But the truly extraordinary suggestion is often made that this escape from the home is an escape into greater freedom. The change is actually offered as favourable to liberty.

To anybody who can think, of course, it is exactly the opposite. The domestic division of human society is not perfect, being human. It does not achieve complete liberty; a thing somewhat difficult to do or even to define. But it is a mere matter of arithmetic that it puts a larger number of people in supreme control of something, and able to shape it to their personal liking, than do the vast organisations that rule society outside; whether those systems are legal or commercial or even merely social.

Even if we were only considering the parents, it is plain that there are more parents than there are policemen or politicians or heads of big businesses or proprietors of hotels. As I shall suggest in a moment, the argument actually applies indirectly to the children as well as directly to the parents. But the main point is that the world OUTSIDE the home is now under a rigid discipline and routine and it is only inside the home that there is really a place for individuality and liberty. Anyone stepping out of the front-door is obliged to step into a procession, all going the same way and to a great extent even obliged to wear the same uniform. Business, especially big business, is now organised like an army. It is, as some would say, a sort of mild militarism without bloodshed; as I should say, a militarism without the military virtues. But anyhow, it is obvious that a hundred clerks in a bank or a hundred waitresses in a teashop are more regimented and under rule than the same individuals when each has gone back to his or her own dwelling or lodging, hung with his or her favourite pictures or fragrant with his or her favourite cheap cigarettes.

But this, which is so obvious in the commercial case, is no less true even in the social case. In practice, the pursuit of pleasure is merely the pursuit of fashion. The pursuit of fashion is merely the pursuit of convention; only that it happens to be a new convention. The jazz dances, the joy rides, the big pleasure parties and hotel entertainments, do not make any more provision for a REALLY independent taste than did any of the fashions of the past. If a wealthy young lady wants to do what all the other wealthy young ladies are doing, she will find it great fun, simply because youth is fun and society is fun. She will enjoy being modern exactly as her Victorian grandmother enjoyed being Victorian. And quite right too; but it is the enjoyment of convention, not the enjoyment of liberty.

It is perfectly healthy for all young people of all historic periods to herd together, to a reasonable extent, and enthusiastically copy each other. But in that there is nothing particularly fresh and certainly nothing particularly free. The girl who likes shaving her head and powdering her nose and wearing short skirts will find the world organised for her and will march happily with the procession. But a girl who happened to like having her hair down to her heels or loading herself with barbaric gauds and trailing garments or (most awful of all) leaving her nose in its natural state--she will still be well advised to do these things on her own premises. If the Duchess does want to play leap frog, she must not start suddenly leaping in the manner of a frog across the ballroom of the Babylon Hotel, when it is crowded with the fifty best couples professionally practising the very latest dance, for the instruction of society. The Duchess will find it easier to practise leap frog to the admiration of her intimate friends in the old oak-panelled hall of Fitzdragon Castle. If the Dean must stand on his head, he will do it with more ease and grace in the calm atmosphere of the Deanery than by attempting to interrupt the programme of some social entertainment already organised for philanthropic purposes.

If there is this impersonal routine in commercial and even in social things, it goes without saying that it exists and always must exist in political and legal things. For instance, the punishments of the State must be sweeping generalisations. It is only the punishments of the home that can possibly be adapted to the individual case; because it is only there that the judge can know anything of the individual. If Tommy takes a silver thimble out of a work-basket, his mother may act very differently according as she knows that he did it for fun or for spite or to sell to somebody, or to get somebody into trouble. But if Tomkins takes a silver thimble out of a shop, the law not only can but must punish him according to the rule made for all shoplifters or stealers of silver. It is only the domestic discipline that can show any sympathy or especially any humour.

I do not say that the family always does do this; but I say that the State never ought to attempt it. So that even if we consider the parents alone as independent princes, and the children merely as subjects, the relative freedom of the family can and often does work to the advantage of those subjects. But so long as the children are children, they will always be the subjects of somebody. The question is whether they are to be distributed naturally under their natural princes, as the old phrase went, who normally feel for them what nobody else will feel, a natural affection. It seems to me clear that this normal distribution gives the largest amount of liberty to the largest number of people.

My complaint of the anti-domestic drift is that it is unintelligent. People do not know what they are doing; because they do not know what they are undoing. There are a multitude of modern manifestations, from the largest to the smallest, ranging from a divorce to a picnic party. But each is a separate escape or evasion; and especially an evasion of the point at issue. People ought to decide in a philosophical fashion whether they desire the traditional social order or not; or if there is any particular alternative to be desired. As it is they treat the public question merely as a mess or medley of private questions.

Even in being anti-domestic they are much too domestic in their test of domesticity. Each family considers only its own case and the result is merely narrow and negative. Each case is an exception to a rule that does not exist. The family, especially in the modern state, stands in need of considerable correction and reconstruction; most things do in the modern state. But the family mansion should be preserved or destroyed or rebuilt; it should not be allowed to fall to pieces brick by brick because nobody has any historic sense of the object of bricklaying.

For instance, the architects of the restoration should rebuild the house with wide and easily opened doors, for the practice of the ancient virtue of hospitality. In other words, private property should be distributed with sufficiently decent equality to allow of a margin for festive intercourse. But the hospitality of a house will always be different from the hospitality of a hotel. And it will be different in being more individual, more independent, more interesting than the hospitality of a hotel.

It is perfectly right that the young Browns and the young Robinsons should meet and mix and dance and make asses of themselves, according to the design of their Creator. But there will always be some difference between the Browns entertaining the Robinsons and the Robinsons entertaining the Browns. And it will be a difference to the advantage of variety, of personality, of the potentialities of the mind of man; or, in other words, of life, liberty and the pursuit of happiness.

The Book of Job

GKC as MC **(1929)**

"The riddles of God are more satisfying than the solutions of man."

I WANTED TO get one essay in here with Chesterton talking directly about scripture. It's exciting to see such a unique mind unpack one of the oldest stories in the Bible. Chesterton sees Job as proof of his message that paradox and the Riddles of God are a much more beautiful reality than the closed systems and monomaniacal philosophies of the rationalists and skeptics.

The problem with any unbeliever is that they are not skeptical enough. If you truly question everything, you come to a place of complete wonder. It's perhaps the closest we can get to the innocent curiosity Adam and Eve must have felt on their first days in existence. And we will have some idea why God told them not to eat from the Tree of the Knowledge of Good and Evil. The moment we try to unravel and rationalize the great mystery of God's creation, we tie ourselves up in tight little knots.

THE BOOK OF JOB is among the other Old Testament books both a philosophical riddle and a historical riddle. It is the philosophical riddle that concerns us in such an introduction as this; so we may dismiss first the few words of general explanation or warning which should be said about the historical aspect. Controversy has long raged about which parts of this epic belong to its original scheme and which are interpolations of considerably later date. The doctors disagree, as it is the business of doctors to do; but upon the whole the trend of investigation has always been in the direction of maintaining that the parts interpolated, if any, were the prose prologue and epilogue, and possibly the speech of the young man who comes in with an apology at the end. I do not profess to be competent to decide such questions.

But whatever decision the reader may come to concerning them, there is a general truth to be remembered in this connection. When you deal with any ancient artistic creation, do not suppose that it is anything against it that it grew gradually. The book of Job may have grown gradually just as Westminster Abbey grew gradually. But the people who made the old folk poetry, like the people who made Westminster Abbey, did not attach that importance to the actual date and the actual author, that importance which is entirely the creation of the almost insane individualism of modern times. We may put aside the case of Job, as one complicated with religious difficulties, and take any other, say the case of the Iliad. Many people have maintained the characteristic formula of modern skepticism, that Homer was not written by Homer, but by another person of the same name. Just in the same way many have maintained that Moses was not Moses but another person called Moses.

But the thing really to be remembered in the matter of the Iliad is that if other people did interpolate the passages, the thing did not create the same sense of shock as would be created by such proceedings in these individualistic times. The creation of the tribal epic was to some extent regarded as a tribal work, like the building of the tribal temple. Believe then, if you will, that the prologue of Job and the epilogue and the speech of Elihu[1] are things inserted after the original work was composed. But do not suppose that such insertions have that obvious and spurious character which would belong to any insertions in a modern, individualistic book.

Without going into questions of unity as understood by the scholars, we may say of the scholarly riddle that the book has unity in the sense that all great traditional creations have unity; in the sense that Canterbury Cathedral has unity[2]. And the same is broadly true of what I have called the philosophical riddle. There is a real sense in which the book of Job stands apart from most of the books included in the canon of the Old Testament. But here again those are wrong who insist on the entire absence of unity. Those are wrong who maintain that the Old Testament is a mere loose library; that it has no consistency or aim. Whether the result was achieved by some supernal spriritual truth, or by a steady national tradition, or merely by an ingenious selection in aftertimes, the books of the Old Testament have a quite perceptible unity.

---

1. Refresher: Elihu is the rando that pops up in Job and gives a super long speech even though he wasn't even one of Job's original friends mentioned in chapter 2. He's like that annoying guy who pops in at the pub when you and your old friends are trying to catch up, but he won't shut up.

While the others argue that trials are signs of sin in someone's life, Elihu says trials can be used to improve us. Or something like that.

Some scholars believe Elihu is the actual author of Job.

2. Canterbury Cathedral was founded in 597. The cathedral was completely rebuilt between 1070 and 1077. The east end was greatly enlarged at the beginning of the 12th century and largely rebuilt in the Gothic style following a fire in 1174, with significant eastward extensions to accommodate the flow of pilgrims visiting the shrine of Thomas Becket, the archbishop who was murdered in the cathedral in 1170. The Norman nave and transepts survived until the late 14th century when they were demolished to make way for the present structures.

In short: the amazing cathedral was built by thousands of people of different eras, added to, destroyed, rebuilt, and upgraded constantly since it was first constructed.

The central idea of the great part of the Old Testament may be called the idea of the loneliness of God. God is not the only chief character of the Old Testament; God is properly the only character in the Old Testament. Compared with His clearness of purpose, all the other wills are heavy and automatic, like those of animals; compared with His actuality, all the sons of flesh are shadows. Again and again the note is struck, "With whom hath He taken counsel?" (Isa. 40:14). "I have trodden the winepress alone, and of the peoples there was no man with me" (Isa. 63:3). All the patriarchs and prophets are merely His tools or weapons; for the Lord is a man of war. He uses Joshua like an axe or Moses like a measuring rod. For Him, Samson, is only a sword and Isaiah a trumpet. The saints of Christianity are supposed to be like God, to be, as it were, little statuettes of Him. The Old Testament hero is no more supposed to be of the same nature as God than a saw or a hammer is supposed to be of the same shape as the carpenter.

This is the main key and characteristic of Hebrew scriptures as a whole. There are, indeed, in those scriptures innumerable instances of the sort of rugged humor, keen emotion, and powerful individuality which is never wanting in great primitive prose and poetry. Nevertheless the main characteristic remains: the sense not merely that God is stronger than man, not merely that God is more secret than man, but that He means more, that He knows better what He is doing, that compared with Him we have something of the vagueness, the unreason, and the vagrancy of the beasts that perish. "It is He that sitteth above the earth, and the inhabitants thereof are as grasshoppers" (Isa.40:22). We might almost put it thus. The book is so intent upon asserting the personality of God that it almost asserts the impersonality of man. Unless this gigantic cosmic brain has conceived a thing, that thing is insecure and void; man has not enough tenacity to ensure its continuance. "Except the Lord build the house, they labor in vain that build it. Except the Lord keep the city, the watchman waketh but in vain" (Ps. 127:1).

Everywhere else, then, the Old Testament positively rejoices in the obliteration of man in comparison with the divine purpose. The book of Job stands definitely alone because the book of Job definitely asks, "But what is the purpose of God? Is it worth the sacrifice even of our miserable humanity? Of course, it is easy enough to wipe out our own paltry wills for the sake of a will that is grander and kinder. But is it grander and kinder? Let God use His tools; let God break His tools. But what is He doing, and what are they being broken for?" It is because of this question that we have to attack as a philosophical riddle the riddle of the book of Job.

The present importance of the book of Job cannot be expressed adequately even by saying that it is the most interesting of ancient books. We may almost say of the book of Job that it is the most interesting of modern books. In truth, of course, neither of the two phrases covers the matter, because fundamental human religion and fundamental human irreligion are both at once old and new; philosophy is either eternal or it is not philosophy. The modern habit of saying "This is my opinion, but I may be wrong" is entirely irrational. If I say that it may be wrong, I say that is not my opinion. The modern habit of saying "Every man has a different philosophy; this is my philosophy and it suits me" – the habit of saying this is mere weak-mindedness. A cosmic philosophy is not constructed to fit a man; a cosmic philosophy is constructed to fit a cosmos. A man can no more possess a private religion than he can possess a private sun and moon.

The first of the intellectual beauties of the book of Job is that it is all concerned with this desire to know the actuality; the desire to know what is, and not merely what seems. If moderns were writing the book, we should probably find that Job and his comforters got on quite well together by the simple operation of referring their differences to what is called the temperament, saying that the comforters were by nature "optimists" and Job by nature a "pessimist." And they would be quite comfortable, as people can often be, for some time at least, by agreeing to say what is obviously untrue. For if the word "pessimist" means anything at all, then emphatically Job is not a pessimist. His case alone is sufficient to refute the modern absurdity of referring everything to physical temperament.

Job does not in any sense look at life in a gloomy way. If wishing to be happy and being quite ready to be happy constitutes an optimist, Job is an optimist. He is a perplexed optimist; he is an exasperated optimist; he is an outraged and insulted optimist. He wishes the universe to justify itself, not because he wishes it be caught out, but because he really wishes it be justified. He demands an explanation from God, but he does not do it at all in the spirit in which Hampden[3] might demand an explanation from Charles I. He does it in the spirit in which a wife might demand an explanation from her husband whom she really respected. He remonstrates with his Maker because he is proud of his Maker. He even speaks of the Almighty as his enemy, but he never doubts, at the back of his mind, that his enemy has some kind of a case which he does not understand.

In a fine and famous blasphemy he says, "Oh, that mine adversary had written a book!" (31:35). It never really occurs to him that it could possibly be a bad book. He is anxious to be convinced, that is, he thinks that God could convince him. In short, we may say again that if the word optimist means anything (which I doubt), Job is an optimist. He shakes the pillars of the world and strikes insanely at the heavens; he lashes the stars, but it is not to silence them; it is to make them speak.

In the same way we may speak of the official optimists, the comforters of Job. Again, if the word pessimist means anything (which I doubt), the comforters of Job may be called pessimists rather than optimists. All that they really believe is not that God is good but that God is so strong that it is much more judicious to call Him good. It would be the exaggeration of censure to call them evolutionists; but they have something of the vital error of the evolutionary optimist. They will keep on saying that everything in the universe fits into everything else; as if there were anything comforting about a number of nasty things all fitting into each other. We shall see later how

---

3. John Hampden was an English landowner and politician whose opposition to arbitrary taxes imposed by Charles I made him a national figure. An ally of Parliamentarian leader John Pym, and cousin to Oliver Cromwell, he was one of the Five Members whose attempted arrest in January 1642 sparked the First English Civil War.

God in the great climax of the poem turns this particular argument altogether upside down.

When, at the end of the poem, God enters (somewhat abruptly), is struck the sudden and splendid note which makes the thing as great as it is.

All the human beings through the story, and Job especially, have been asking questions of God. A more trivial poet would have made God enter in some sense or other in order to answer the questions. By a touch truly to be called inspired, when God enters, it is to ask a number of questions on His own account. In this drama of skepticism God Himself takes up the role of skeptic. He does what all the great voices defending religion have always done. He does, for instance, what Socrates did. He turns rationalism against itself. He seems to say that if it comes to asking questions, He can ask some question which will fling down and flatten out all conceivable human questioners.

The poet by an exquisite intuition has made God ironically accept a kind of controversial equality with His accusers. He is willing to regard it as if it were a fair intellectual duel: "Gird up now thy loins like man; for I will demand of thee, and answer thou me" (38:3). The everlasting adopts an enormous and sardonic humility. He is quite willing to be prosecuted. He only asks for the right which every prosecuted person possesses; he asks to be allowed to cross-examine the witness for the prosecution. And He carries yet further the corrections of the legal parallel. For the first question, essentially speaking, which He asks of Job is the question that any criminal accused by Job would be most entitled to ask. He asks Job who he is. And Job, being a man of candid intellect, takes a little time to consider, and comes to the conclusion that he does not know.

This is the first great fact to notice about the speech of God, which is the culmination of the inquiry. It represents all human skeptics routed by a higher skepticism.

It is this method, used sometimes by supreme and sometimes by mediocre minds, that has ever since been the logical weapon of the true mystic.

153

Socrates, as I have said, used it when he showed that if you only allowed him enough sophistry he could destroy all sophists[4]. Jesus Christ used it when he reminded the Sadducees, who could not imagine the nature of marriage in heaven, that if it came to that they had not really imagined the nature of marriage at all. In the break up of Christian theology in the eighteenth century, Butler[5] used it, when he pointed out that rationalistic arguments could be used as much against vague religions as against doctrinal religion, as much against rationalist ethics as against Christian ethics. It is the root and reason of the fact that men who have religious faith have also philosophic doubt. These are the small streams of the delta; the book of Job is the first great cataract that creates the river. In dealing with the arrogant asserter of doubt, it is not the right method to tell him to stop doubting. It is rather the right method to tell him to go on doubting , to doubt a little more, to doubt every day newer and wilder things in the universe, until at last, by some strange enlightenment, he may begin to doubt himself.

This, I say, is the first fact touching the speech; the fine inspiration by which God comes in at the end, not to answer riddles, but to propound them. The other great fact which, taken together with this one, makes the whole work religious instead of merely philosophical is that other great surprise which makes Job suddenly satisfied with the mere presentation of something impenetrable. Verbally speaking the enigmas of Jehovah seem darker and more desolate than the enigmas of Job; yet Job was comfortless before the speech of Jehovah and is comforted after it. He has been told nothing, but he feels the terrible and tingling atmosphere of something which is too good to be told. The refusal of God to explain His design is itself a burning hint of His design. The riddles of God are more satisfying than the solutions of man.

---

4. The Sophists held no values other than winning and succeeding. They were not true believers in the myths of the Greeks but would use references and quotations from the tales for their own purposes. They were secular atheists, relativists and cynical about religious beliefs and all traditions.

5. Joseph Butler was an English Anglican bishop, theologian, apologist, and philosopher. He was born in Wantage in the English county of Berkshire (now Oxfordshire). He is known, among other things, for his critique of Deism, Thomas Hobbes's egoism, and John Locke's theory of personal identity. Butler influenced many philosophers and religious thinkers, including David Hume, Thomas Reid, Adam Smith, Henry Sidgwick, John Henry Newman, and C. D. Broad, and is widely considered "as one of the preeminent English moralists."

Thirdly, of course, it is one of the splendid strokes that God rebukes alike the man who accused and the men who defended Him; that He knocks down pessimists and optimists with the same hammer. And it is in connection with the mechanical and supercilious comforters of Job that there occurs the still deeper and finer inversion of which I have spoken. The mechanical optimist endeavors to justify the universe avowedly upon the ground that it is a rational and consecutive pattern. He points out that the fine thing about the world is that it can all be explained. That is the one point, if I may put it so, on which God, in return, is explicit to the point of violence. God says, in effect, that if there is one fine thing about the world, as far as men are concerned, it is that it cannot be explained. He insists on the inexplicableness of everything. "Hath the rain a father?. . .Out of whose womb came the ice?" (38:28f). He goes farther, and insists on the positive and palpable unreason of things; "Hast thou sent the rain upon the desert where no man is, and upon the wilderness wherein there is no man?" (38:26).

God will make man see things, if it is only against the black background of nonentity. God will make Job see a startling universe if He can only do it by making Job see an idiotic universe. To startle man, God becomes for an instant a blasphemer; one might almost say that God becomes for an instant an atheist. He unrolls before Job a long panorama of created things, the horse, the eagle, the raven, the wild ass, the peacock, the ostrich, the crocodile. He so describes each of them that it sounds like a monster walking in the sun. The whole is a sort of psalm or rhapsody of the sense of wonder. The maker of all things is astonished at the things he has Himself made.

This we may call the third point. Job puts forward a note of interrogation; God answers with a note of exclamation. Instead of proving to Job that it is an explicable world, He insists that it is a much stranger world than Job ever thought it was. Lastly, the poet has achieved in this speech, with that unconscious artistic accuracy found in so many of the simpler epics, another and much more delicate thing. Without once relaxing the rigid impenetrability of Jehovah in His deliberate declaration, he has contrived to let fall here and there in the metaphors, in the parenthetical imagery, sudden and splendid suggestions that the secret of God is a bright and not a sad one – semi-accidental suggestions, like light seen for an instant through the crack of a closed door.

It would be difficult to praise too highly, in a purely poetical sense, the instinctive exactitude and ease with which these more optimistic insinuations are let fall in other connections, as if the Almighty Himself were scarcely aware that He was letting them out. For instance, there is that famous passage where Jehovah, with devastating sarcasm, asks Job where he was when the foundations of the world were laid, and then (as if merely fixing a date) mentions the time when the sons of God shouted for joy (38:4-7). One cannot help feeling, even upon this meager information, that they must have had something to shout about. Or again, when God is speaking of snow and hail in the mere catalogue of the physical cosmos, he speaks of them as a treasury that He has laid up against the day of battle – a hint of some huge Armageddon in which evil shall be at last overthrown.

Nothing could be better, artistically speaking, than this optimism breaking though agnosticism like fiery gold round the edges of a black cloud. Those who look superficially at the barbaric origin of the epic may think it fanciful to read so much artistic significance into its casual similes or accidental phrases. But no one who is well acquainted with great examples of semi-barbaric poetry, as in The Song of Roland[6] or the old ballads, will fall into this mistake. No one who knows what primitive poetry is can fail to realize that while its conscious form is simple some of its finer effects are subtle. The Iliad contrives to express the idea that Hector and Sarpedon have a certain tone or tint of sad and chivalrous resignation, not bitter enough to be called pessimism and not jovial enough to be called optimism; Homer could never have said this in elaborate words. But somehow he contrives to say it in simple words. The Song of Roland contrives to express the idea that Christianity imposes upon its heroes a paradox; a paradox of great humility in the matter of their sins combined with great ferocity in the matter of their ideas. Of course The Song of Roland could not say this; but it conveys this. In the same way, the book of Job must be credited with many subtle effects which were in the author's soul without being, perhaps, in the author's mind. And of these by far the most important remains to be stated.

I do not know, and I doubt whether even scholars know, if the book of Job had a great effect or had any effect upon the after development of Jewish thought. But if it did have any effect it may have saved them from an enormous collapse and decay. Here in this book the question is really asked whether God invariably punishes vice with terrestrial

6. An 11th-century epic poem based on Roland and the Battle of Roncevaux Pass in 778, during the reign of Charlemagne. It is the oldest surviving major work of French literature and exists in various manuscript versions, which testify to its enormous and enduring popularity from the 12th to 16th centuries.

punishment and rewards virtue with terrestrial prosperity. If the Jews had answered that question wrongly they might have lost all their after influence in human history. They might have sunk even down to the level of modern well-educated society. For when once people have begun to believe that prosperity is the reward of virtue, their next calamity is obvious. If prosperity is regarded as the reward of virtue it will be regarded as the symptom of virtue. Men will leave off the heavy task of making good men successful. He will adopt the easier task of making out successful men good. This, which has happened throughout modern commerce and journalism, is the ultimate Nemesis of the wicked optimism of the comforters of Job. If the Jews could be saved from it, the book of Job saved them.

The book of Job is chiefly remarkable, as I have insisted throughout, for the fact that it does not end in a way that is conventionally satisfactory. Job is not told that his misfortunes were due to his sins or a part of any plan for his improvement. But in the prologue we see Job tormented not because he was the worst of men, but because he was the best. It is the lesson of the whole work that man is most comforted by paradoxes. Here is the very darkest and strangest of the paradoxes; and it is by all human testimony the most reassuring. I need not suggest what high and strange history awaited this paradox of the best man in the worst fortune. I need not say that in the freest and most philosophical sense there is one Old Testament figure who is truly a type; or say what is prefigured in the wounds of Job.

What is Right With the World

T.P.'s Weekly **(1910)**

"What is right with the world is the world. In fact, nearly everything
else is wrong with it."

I'M ENDING WITH this fairly uplifting chapter because I think it is a good counter attack to the barrage of politics and calls for unity, revolution, and progress that we hear day in and day out. A reminder that man is not going to save the world, man is the one who ruined it and the goodness of man, of this Earth, and of existence, existed from day one and is—for the most part—available to us still.

I love that Chesterton challenges the idea of uniting as an inherent good—an idea our culture takes for granted as unquestionably good. Jackals can unite to tear you apart, thieves can unite to pull off a heist. Multiple forest fires can unite and create a mass inferno. "Unity" is one of those words, much like "progress" or "forward-thinking," that actually says nothing

159

about morality and yet is always used as a moral bludgeon. People like to use these words because they can mean anything even though they carry no actual weight.

It is useful to sit down and remember that this creation is good, and nobody expresses it better than Chesterton.

THE ABOVE EXCELLENT title is not of my own invention. It was suggested to me by the Editor of this paper (T.P.'s Weekly), and I consented to fill up the bill, partly because of the pleasure I have always had from the paper itself, and partly because it gives me an opportunity of telling an egotistical story, a story which may enlighten the public about the general origin of such titles.

I have always heard of the brutality of publishers and how they crush and obscure the author; but my complaint has always been that they push him forward far too much. I will not say that, so far from making too little of the author, they make too much of him; that this phrase is capable of a dark financial interpretation which I do not intend. But I do say that the prominent personalities of the literary world are very largely the creations of their publishers, in so far as they are not solely the creations of their wives.

Here is a small incident out of my own existence. I designed to write a sort of essay, divided into sections, on one particular point of political error. This fallacy, though small and scholastic at first sight, seemed to me to be the real mistake in most modern sociological works. It was, briefly, the idea that things that have been tried have been found wanting. It was my purpose to point out that in the entanglements of practice this is untrue; that an old expedient may be the best thing for a new situation; that its principle may be useful though its practice was abandoned; and so on.

Therefore, I claimed, we should look for the best method, the ideal, whether it is in the future or the past. I imagined this book as a drab-coloured,

decorous little philosophical treatise, with no chapters, but the page occasion-
ally broken by section-headings at the side. I proposed to call my analysis of
a radical error 'What is wrong', meaning where the mistake is in our logical
calculation. But I had highly capable and sympathetic publishers, whose
only weakness was that they thought my unhappy monologue much more
important than I did. By some confusion of ecstasy (which entirely through
my own fault I failed to check) the title was changed into the apocalyptic
trumpet-blast 'What's Wrong With the World'. It was divided up into three
short, fierce chapters, like proclamations in a French riot. Outside there was
an enormous portrait of myself looking like a depressed hairdresser, and the
whole publication had somehow got the violence and instancy of a bombshell.
Let it be understood that I do not blame the publishers in the least for this. I
could have stopped it if I had minded my own affairs, and came out of their
beautiful and ardent souls. I merely mention it as an instance of the error
about publishers. They are always represented as cold and scornful merchants,
seeking to keep your writers in the background. Alas (as Wordsworth so finely
says), alas! the enthusiasm of publishers has oftener left me mourning.

Upon the whole, I am rather inclined to approve of this method of the
publisher or editor making up the title, while the author makes up the remarks about it. Any man with a large mind ought to be able to write about
anything. Any really free man ought to be able to write to order. Some of the
greatest books in the world -- Pickwick[1], for instance -- were written to fulfil a
scheme partly sketched out by a publisher. But I only brought together these
two cases of title that came to me from outside because they do illustrate the
necessity of some restatement in such a case. For these two titles are, when it
comes to the fulfilment, at once too complex and too simple.

I would never have dreamed of announcing, like some discovery of my
own, what is wrong with the world. What is wrong with the world is the devil,

---

1. The Posthumous Papers of the Pickwick Club (also known as The Pickwick Papers) was Charles Dickens'
first novel. Dickens was asked by the publisher Chapman & Hall to supply descriptions to explain a series
of comic "cockney sporting plates" by illustrator Robert Seymour, and to connect them into a novel. The
book became Britain's first real publishing phenomenon, with bootleg copies, theatrical performances, joke
books, and other merchandise. Published in 19 issues over 20 months, the success of The Pickwick Papers
popularised serialised fiction and cliffhanger endings.

and what is right with it is God; the human race will travel for a few more million years in all sorts of muddle and reform, and when it perishes of the last cold or heat it will still be within the limits of that very simple defini- tion. But in an age that has confused itself with such phrases as 'optimist' and 'pessimist', it is necessary to distinguish along more delicate lines. One of the strangest things about the use of the word 'optimist' is that it is now so con- stantly used about the future. The house of man is criticised not as a house, but as a kind of caravan; not by what it is, but by where it is going. None are more vitally and recklessly otherworldly than those modern progressives who do not believe in another world.

Now, for the matter of that, I do not think the world is getting much better in very many vital respects. In some of them, I think, the fact could hardly be disputed. The one perfectly satisfactory element at the present crisis is that all the prophecies have failed. At least the people who have been clearly proved to be wrong are the people who were quite sure they were right. That is always a gratifying circumstance. Now why is it that all these prophecies of the wise have been confounded and why has the destiny of men taken so decisive and different a course? It is because of the very simple fact that the human race consists of many millions of two-legged and tolerably cheerful, reasonably unhappy beings who never read any books at all and certainly never hear of any scientific predictions. If they act in opposition to the scheme which science has foreseen for them, they must be excused. They sin in ignorance. They have no notion that they are avoiding what was really unavoidable.

But, indeed, the phrases loosely used of that obscure mass of mankind are a little misleading. To say of the bulk of human beings that they are un- educated is like saying of a Red Indian hunter that he has not yet taken his degree. He has taken many other things. And so, sincerely speaking, there are no uneducated men. They may escape the trivial examinations, but not the tremendous examinations of existence. The dependence of infancy, the enjoyment of animals, the love of woman and the fear of death -- these are more frightful and more fixed than all conceivable forms of the cultivation of the mind. It is idle to complain of schools and colleges being trivial. In no case will a college ever teach the important things. He has learnt them right or wrong, and he has learnt them all alone.

We therefore come back to the primary truth, that what is right with the world has nothing to do with future changes, but is rooted in original realities. If groups or peoples show an unexpected independence or creative power; if they do things no one had dreamed of their doing; if they prove more ferocious or more self-sacrificing than the wisdom of the world had ever given them credit for, then such inexplicable outbursts can always be referred back to some elementary and absolute doctrine about the nature of men.

No traditions in this world are so ancient as the traditions that lead to modern upheaval and innovation. Nothing nowadays is so conservative as a revolution. The men who call themselves Republicans are men walking the streets of deserted and tiny city-states, and digging up the great bones of pagans. And when we ask on what republicanism really rests, we come back to that great indemonstrable dogma of the native dignity of man. And when we come back to the lord of creation, we come back of necessity to creation; and we ask ourselves that ultimate question which St Thomas Aquinas (an extreme optimist) answered in the affirmative: Are these things ultimately of value at all?

What is right with the world is the world. In fact, nearly everything else is wrong with it. This is that great truth in the tremendous tale of Creation, a truth that our people must remember or perish. It is at the beginning that things are good, and not (as the more pallid progressives say) only at the end. The primordial things -- existence, energy, fruition -- are good so far as they go. You cannot have evil life, though you can have notorious evil livers. Manhood and womanhood are good things, though men and women are often perfectly pestilent. You can use poppies to drug people, or birch trees to beat them, stone to make an idol, or corn to make a corner; but it remains true that, in the abstract, before you have done anything, each of these four things is in strict truth a glory, a beneficent speciality and variety.

We do praise the Lord that there are birch trees growing amongst the rocks and poppies amongst the corn; we do praise the Lord, even if we do not believe in Him. We do admire and applaud the project of a world, just as if we had been called to council in the primal darkness and seen the first starry plan of the skies. We are, as a matter of fact, far more certain that this life of ours is a magnificent and amazing enterprise than we are that it will succeed. These evolutionary optimists who called themselves Meliorists[2] (a patient and poor-spirited lot they are) always talk as if we were certain of the end, though not of the beginning. In other words, they don't know what life is aiming at, but they are quite sure it will get there. Why anybody who has avowedly forgotten where he came from should be quite so certain of where he is going to I have never been able to make out; but Meliorists are like that. They are ready to talk of existence itself as the product of purely evil forces. They never mention animals except as perpetually tearing each other to pieces; but a month in the country would cure that. They have a real giddy horror of stars and seas, as a man has on the edge of a hopelessly high precipice. They sometimes instinctively shrink from clay, fungoids, and the fresh young of animals with a quivering gesture that reveals the fundamental pessimist. Life itself, crude, uncultivated life, is horrible to them. They belong very largely to the same social class and creed as the lady who objected that the milk came to her from a dirty cow, and not from a nice clean shop. But they are sure how everything will end.

I am in precisely the opposite position. I am much more sure that everything is good at the beginning than I am that everything will be good at the end. That all this frame of things, this flesh, these stones, are good things, of that I am more brutally certain than I can say. But as for what will happen to them, that is to take a step into dogma and prophecy. I speak here, of course, solely of my personal feelings, not even of my reasoned creed. But on my instincts alone I should have no notion what would ultimately happen to this material world I think so magnificent. For all I know it may be literally

2. Meliorism: The belief that the human condition can be improved through concerted effort and that there is an inherent tendency toward progress or improvement in the human condition.

and not figuratively true that the tares are tied into bundles for burning, and that as the tree falleth so shall it lie.

I am an agnostic, like most people with a positive theology. But I do affirm, with the full weight of sincerity, that trees and flowers are good at the beginning, whatever happens to them at the end; that human lives were good at the beginning, whatever happens to them in the end. The ordinary modern progressive position is that this is a bad universe, but will certainly get better. I say it is certainly a good universe, even if it gets worse. I say that these trees and flowers, stars and sexes, are primarily, not merely ultimately, good. In the Beginning the power beyond words created heaven and earth. In the Beginning He looked on them and saw that they were good.

All this unavoidable theory (for theory is always unavoidable) may be popularly pulled together thus. We are to regard existence as a raid or great adventure; it is to be judged, therefore, not by what calamities it encounters, but by what flag it follows and what high town it assaults. The most danger-ous thing in the world is to be alive; one is always in danger of one's life. But anyone who shrinks from this is a traitor to the great scheme and experiment of being. The pessimist of the ordinary type, the pessimist who thinks he would be better dead, is blasted with the crime of Iscariot.[3] Spiritually speak-ing, we should be justified in punishing him with death. Only, out of polite deference to his own philosophy, we punish him with life.

But this faith (that existence was fundamentally and purposely good) is not attacked only by the black, consistent pessimist. The man who says that he would sooner die is best answered by a sudden blow with the poker, for the reply is rightly logical, as well as physically very effective. But there has crept through the culture of modern Europe another notion that is equally in its own way an attack on the essential rightness of the world. It is not avowedly pessimistic, though the source from which it comes (which is Buddhism) is pessimistic for those who really understand it. It can offer itself — as it does

---

3. You know, the guy who betrayed Jesus. First name Judas, last name Iscariot, middle name huge jerk.

among some of the high-minded and distinguished Theosophists[4]— with an air of something highly optimistic. But this disguised pessimism is what is really wrong with the world — at least, especially with the modern world. It is essential to arrest and to examine it.

There has crept into our thoughts, through a thousand small openings, a curious and unnatural idea. I mean the idea that unity is itself a good thing; that there is something high and spiritual about things being blended and absorbed into each other. That all rivers should run into one river, that all vegetables should go into one pot -- that is spoken of as the last and best fulfilment of being. Boys are to be 'at one' with girls; all sects are to be 'at one' in the New Theology; beasts fade into men and men fade into God; union in itself is a noble thing.

Now union in itself is not a noble thing. Love is a noble thing; but love is not union. Nay, it is rather a vivid sense of separation and identity. Maudlin[5], inferior love poetry does, indeed, talk of lovers being 'one soul', just as maudlin, inferior religious poetry talks of being lost in God; but the best poetry does not. When Dante meets Beatrice[6], he feels his distance from her, not his proximity; and all the greatest saints have felt their lowness, not their highness, in the moment of ecstasy. And what is true of these grave and heroic matters (I do not say, of course, that saints and lovers have never used the language of union too, true enough in its own place and proper limitation of meaning) -- what is true of these is equally true of all the lighter and less essential forms of appreciation of surprise. Division and variety are essential to praise; division and variety are what is right with the world. There is nothing specially right about mere contact and coalescence.

---

4. Theosophy teaches that the purpose of human life is spiritual emancipation and claims that the human soul undergoes reincarnation upon bodily death according to a process of karma. It promotes values of universal brotherhood and social improvement, although it does not stipulate particular ethical codes.

5. Hey, I didn't know what this word meant so I'm footnoting it.

Maudlin: self-pityingly or tearfully sentimental, often through drunkenness.

6. Beatrice was a prominent character, representative of divine love in Dante's Divine Comedy, the guide of Heaven — but she was based on a real woman named Beatrice, one who he claims he only met briefly twice in his life, separated by many years and the first time when he was only nine. Apparently he had a massive lifelong crush on her and she probably had no clue.

In short, this vast, vague idea of unity is the one 'reactionary' thing in the world. It is perhaps the only connection in which that foolish word 'reactionary' can be used with significance and truth. For this blending of men and women, nations and nations, is truly a return to the chaos and unconsciousness that were before the world was made. There is of course, another kind of unity of which I do not speak here; unity in the possession of truth and the perception of the need for these varieties. But the varieties themselves; the reflection of man and woman in each other, as in two distinct mirrors; the wonder of man at nature as a strange thing at once above and below him; the quaint and solitary kingdom of childhood; the local affections and the colour of certain landscapes -- these actually are the things that are the grace and honour of the earth; these are the things that make life worth living and the whole framework of things well worthy to be sustained. And the best thing remains; that this view, whether conscious or not, always has been and still is the view of the living and labouring millions.

While a few prigs on platforms are talking about 'oneness' and absorption in 'The All', the folk that dwell in all the valleys of this ancient earth are renewing the varieties for ever. With them a woman is loved for being unmanly, and a man loved for being un-womanly. With them the church and the home are both beautiful, because they are both different; with them fields are personal and flags are sacred; they are the virtue of existence, for they are not mankind but men.

The rooted hope of the modern world is that all these dim democracies do still believe in that romance of life, that variation of man, woman and child upon which all poetry has hitherto been built. The danger of the modern world is that these dim democracies are so very dim, and that they are especially dim where they are right. The danger is that the world may fall under a new oligarchy -- the oligarchy of prigs. And if anyone should promptly ask (in the manner of the debating clubs) for the definition of a prig, I can only reply that a prig is an oligarch who does not even know he is an oligarch.

A circle of small pedants sit on an upper platform, and pass unanimously (in a meeting of none) that there is no difference between the social duties of men and of women, the social instruction of men or of children. Below them boils that multitudinous sea of millions that think differently, that have always thought differently, that will always think differently. In spite of the overwhelming majority that maintains the old theory of life, I am in some real doubt about which will win. Owing to the decay of theology and all the other clear systems of thought, men have been thrown back very much upon their instincts, as with animals. As with animals, their instincts are right; but, as with animals, they can be cowed. Between the agile scholars and the stagnant mob, I am really doubtful about which will be triumphant. I have no doubt at all about which ought to be.

Europe at present exhibits a concentration upon politics which is partly the unfortunate result of our loss of religion, partly the just and needful result of our loss of our social inequality and iniquity. These causes, however, will not remain in operation for ever. Religion is returning from her exile; it is more likely that the future will be crazily and corruptly superstitious than that it will be merely rationalist.

On the other hand, our attempts to right the extreme ill-balance of wealth must soon have some issue; something will be done to lessen the perpetual torture of incompetent compassion; some scheme will be substituted for our malevolent anarchy, if it be only one of benevolent servitude. And as these two special unrests about the universe and the State settle down into more silent and enduring system, there will emerge more and more those primary and archaic truths which the dust of these two conflicts has veiled. The secondary questions relatively solved, we shall find ourselves all the more in the presence of the primary questions of Man.

For at present we all tend to one mistake; we tend to make politics too important. We tend to forget how huge a part of a man's life is the same under a Sultan and a Senate, under Nero or St Louis. Daybreak is a never-ending glory, getting out of bed is a never-ending nuisance; food and friends will be welcomed; work and strangers must be accepted and endured; birds will go bedwards and children won't, to the end of the last evening. And the worst peril is that in our just modern revolt against intolerable accidents we may have unsettled those things that alone make daily life tolerable. It will be an ironic tragedy if, when we have toiled to find rest, we find we are incurably restless. It will be sad if, when we have worked for our holiday, we find we have unlearnt everything but work.

The typical modern man is the insane millionaire who has drudged to get money, and then finds he cannot enjoy even money. There is danger that the social reformer may silently and occultly develop some of the madness of the millionaire whom he denounces. He may find that he has learnt how to build playgrounds but forgotten how to play. He may agitate for peace and quiet, but only propagate his own mental agitation. In his long fight to get a slave a half-holiday he may angrily deny those ancient and natural things, the zest of being, the divinity of man, the sacredness of simple things, the health and humour of the earth, which alone make a half-holiday even half a holiday or a slave even half a man.

There is danger in that modern phrase 'divine discontent'.[7] There is truth in it also, of course; but it is only truth of a special and secondary kind. Much of the quarrel between Christianity and the world has been due to this fact; that there are generally two truths, as it were, at any given moment of revolt or reaction, and the ancient underlying truism which is nevertheless true all the time.

It is sometimes worth while to point out that black is not so black as it is painted; but black is still black, and not white. So with the merits of content and discontent. It is true that in certain acute and painful crises of oppression or disgrace, discontent is a duty and shame could call us like a trumpet. But it is not true that man should look at life with an eye of discontent, however high-minded. It is not true that in his primary, naked relation to the world, in his relation to sex, to pain, to comradeship, to the grave or to the weather, man ought to make discontent his ideal; it is black lunacy. Half his poor little hopes of happiness hang on his thinking a small house pretty, a plain wife charming, a lame foot not unbearable, and bad cards not so bad. The voice of the special rebels and prophets, recommending discontent, should, as I have said, sound now and then suddenly, like a trumpet. But the voices of the saints and sages, recommending contentment, should sound unceasingly, like the sea.

---

7. The idea that not being content with what is will divinely inspire people toward great things such as art, social reform, and innovation to make the world a better place.

Afterword:
The Chestertonians

I WANTED TO do a short section here at the end of this book about starting a Chesterton reading group. Both of the groups I have been in have become known as the Chestertonians. When I started my first group with my friend Doug TenNapel, I had no idea that Chesterton groups were a thing. I had never been part of a book club or reading group. Up to that point I was not particularly a fan of sitting around in a circle and reading out loud. But there is something about Chesterton that makes me want to read him out loud, share him, and discuss his words. I want people to laugh with when he makes his playfully absurd analogies, I want to see if others are as confused as I am when he refers to some old thing or makes some strange analogy, and I want to revel in those moments when he makes a point that seems to digitally remaster my view of my existence.

The other thing I have noticed about Chesterton groups is that they tend to be a really good filter for quality people. Our groups have always been very eclectic. We have everyone from lawyers, film directors, and medical professionals to comedians, artists, and truck drivers. The common thread is that they all have a hunger for intellectual discussion and yet do not take themselves too seriously. Chesterton attracts people who like to laugh as well as learn. People who want to talk history as well as spirituality, politics as well as art. Chesterton wrote about everything, and that is another reason you can read his works in a group and it remains fresh for years. He doesn't continually hammer away at a single topic. He has repeating themes, but his content is incredibly varied.

This isn't to say you might get your occasional conspiracy theorist or wacko flat Earth guy, but they usually weed themselves out.

Our Chesterton groups have always been men's groups. We smokes cigars, share whiskey, and banter between and after chapters. The conversation usually starts with whatever the chapter we read was about, and eventually it veers off into some other random direction. My current group has mostly Protestants, a few Catholics, some Greek Orthodox, and even an occasional Muslim.

I'm not sure how up to date it is, but I believe you can search for Chesterton groups in your area at https://www.chesterton.org/local-societies/

If you have no group, I encourage you to try to start one even with one or two friends. That's what I did. Both of my groups started very small and grew only by private invitation and word of mouth.

Where To Go From Here

SO, NOW THAT you have read a book of introductory essays, I hope you're curious enough to dive into your first full Chesterton book. Here's a list of possible books to start with and some short notes on what to expect. Chesterton wrote massive amounts so there is no way I can cover everything here, but these are some of his most popular books that I have read.

NONFICTION

Orthodoxy: This is Chesterton's explanation of why he is a Christian. He is not laying out a systematic explanation of his faith as we would expect having read something like Mere Christianity or modern apologetics books. Chesterton is laying out his various thought processes and revelations throughout life that, as a sum total, led him to his belief. He's not directly taking on arguments against faith, though sometimes he is. It is important to understand as you read this book, that even if you don't track with some parts, you don't have to. It's not one track. It rarely is with Chesterton. It's more like he is painting you various pictures that, when taken as a whole, add up to make a larger image. This book is beautiful and contains some of Chesterton's most inspired writing. It is a must-read for sure.

And just so you know, Dale Ahlquist, the biggest Chesterton smarty-pants there is, says it takes three reads to really begin to understand *Orthodoxy*.

Heretics: If you want to read them in order, Heretics technically came before *Orthodoxy*. Each chapter takes a thinker of his time such as H.G. Wells or George Bernard Shaw and rebuts their philosophy. *Orthodoxy* was the book he wrote next after he was continually asked, "Well if all these guys are heretical, then what's orthodox?" So he wrote *Orthodoxy*.

Heretics has some excellent chapters. His chapter on the family is one of my all-time favorites and is included in this book. But there are definitely some chapters that are hard to follow in modern times. This book is very contemporary and addresses things that were currently happening in early 1900's English culture. It is definitely worth reading, but may not be a best first book. That said, this was my first book, and I thought it was great. I wanted to read *Orthodoxy*, but felt I had to read them in order. You really don't. There were enough passages to get me hooked even though a large bulk of it confused me.

The Everlasting Man: *The Everlasting Man* is an excellent book, but it's important to note that this book feels much more like a textbook than Chesterton's others. It has some very long chapters and insanely long paragraphs. It's much more dry and historical than much of his other work. He is much less playful in this book.

This book was basically Chesterton's rebuttal of H.G. Well's book *A Short History of the World* and was a big influence on C.S. Lewis coming to faith. It's academic. It has tons of history and can be hard to read if you don't know your history. Try to get a history buff in your Chesterton group if you read this one, it helps a lot. This is definitely a must-read, but just be prepared. It's like a walk through the history of Earth with G.K. Chesterton in a particularly serious mood.

What's Wrong With The World: This is an interesting read where Chesterton takes on many things people considered real progress at the time. The most fascinating part for me was the part about women's suffrage. As usual, Chesterton doesn't come in on one of the two expected sides of the issue, he has a third way in. He takes on other issues of economics and education as well. This book isn't quite as academic as *The Everlasting Man* in my memory—he uses humor more, and the chapters are more essay-like.

Eugenics And Other Evils: I must admit it has been a long time since I read this and I don't recall many specifics, but Chesterton was a lone voice against eugenics in his time. It was all the rage until Hitler went a little too hard on it and it became sort of not cool (though let's face it, Planned Parenthood is still carrying the torch). I remember enjoying this one as a group, and I plan to read it again.

The Autobiography of G.K. Chesterton: I only mention this one because a lot of people think this might be a good place to start. N-n-n-n-oooo don't do it! I love Chesterton with the mightiest of man-crushes, but this is a rough read. Chesterton didn't like talking about himself, so he spends most of the book talking about other people, which is sweet of him, but that's not what you came to the Chesterton autobiography for. Also, you would love to know about his relationship with his wife, but it is never mentioned because apparently she knew he'd make the whole book about her so she forbade him from mentioning her. I have heard of some people who enjoyed this book (psychopaths), but for our reading group it was a real slog.

FICTION

Our first group read a couple of Chesterton's fiction books together. I enjoyed it, but most of the guys seemed to prefer the non-fiction.

The Man Who Was Thursday: The Man Who Was Thursday is probably Chesterton's most well-known fiction novel. It is a lot of fun and has some hilarious moments in it, lots of action and some beautiful writing. That said, by the end, the "How High Was Chesterton?" meter starts to rise quite bit, though I have had people explain to me what he was doing there, and admittedly a lot of things go over my head.

Man Alive: This is a fairly short novel that is a fun read. It is about a large man named Innocent Smith who at first seems to be some kind of psychopath, but as the book goes on... well just read it, it's short and great.

The Ball and the Cross: This is my favorite fiction book of Chesterton's. It's a hilarious buddy comedy about a Catholic Irishmen and a Scottish atheist who have decided to have a duel to the death over their conflicting beliefs. However, every time they try to kill each other, modern society is there to stop them. The two become fugitives on a sort of mad caper across England as all of the insane philosophies attempt to stick them in the madhouse. It's not that long of a book, and it's got a simple premise that just delivers. I really love it and highly recommend it.

Father Brown Mysteries: I admit to only having read a handful of these. Many people love them. They aren't my favorite, though I do enjoy them. They are fairly short so, if you are curious about them, give them a try. I don't remember them well enough to suggest which ones are the best, though I know The Blue Cross was his first Father Brown mystery, so why not start there?

Three more notes to prepare you for being a true G.K. Chesterton fan and not some poser like those other people who only share his quotes:

- **Chesterton's most famous quote is not one he actually said:** "When Man ceases to worship God he does not worship nothing but worships everything." This is actually a combination of Chesterton quotes. The Society of G.K. Chesterton wrote a helpful piece on this famous quote at https://www.chesterton.org/ceases-to-worship/.

- **Also, you may get some neck beard shouting at you that Chesterton was a "renowned anti-semite!"** The Society of G.K. Chesterton goes into great detail debunking this smear at https://www.chesterton.org/was-chesterton-antisemitic/

- **Lastly, the Society of G.K. Chesterton has put together a great reading plan** if you want something more comprehensive and thought out: https://www.chesterton.org/READING-PLAN/

About Ethan Nicolle

Ethan Nicolle first broke into comics when he created two volumes of Chumble Spuzz for SLG Publishing in 2007 which was nominated for an Eisner Award for humor in 2009. He went on to create a web comic called Axe Cop with his little brother that became a viral sensation and went on to become an animated series on FOX and FXX. He has had multiple pitches optioned at Cartoon Network and worked as a staff writer and story editor on VeggieTales in the House and VeggieTales in the City at Dreamworks Animation for NetFlix, writing over 50 episodes. Nicolle has also written on other shows like Teen Titans Go! and Bunnicula. His own books include Bears Want To Kill You: The Authoritative Guide To Survival In The War Between Man And Bear, and the midgrade novel Brave Ollie Possum. He did the book illustrations for Nick Offerman's books Gumption and Good Clean Fun. Ethan Nicolle is the creative director of the Babylon Bee where he writes, creates visuals, hosts the Babylon Bee Podcast, and animates problematic cartoons

Made in the USA
Columbia, SC
09 October 2021